"Amongst Th

My head rested comfortab
In total silence I hear n
Silence is broken as the w.   ends wind
to crash against my skin
So I decide to close my eyes ᴜ   ᴜle
I unclench my fist as my finger   ᴊ feel the freedom
of life
My heart beats the warmth into my soul
A tear of joy streams down my face as I decide to
finally let go
I can smell the scent of my own paradise
My peace,my dream, my existence all collide with the
darkness within sparking a firework display
The colors of who I am escape from my body
None of the troubles exist in this moment
Only the surrender of all I've kept secluded from
myself
The breeze whistles clarity into my spirit
The sky lights up as I open my eyes
Stars spell out my story,my fate
I no longer have to wonder about what's out there in
the endless universe
At that very second I realize we are amongst the
stars

"One Heartbeat"

In your beautiful eyes I see who I need
That look you give me that sets me free
Just with that look you made the blind side of me
see
With only that look you made my dead heart beat

From your amazing lips you say words I need to
survive
Those words that you say that convince me to strive
Just with those words you make me thrive
With only these words you make my lost soul come
alive

I wonder how you find your way into my dreams
You're so far away but always with me it seems
Holding my hand under starry skies beside running
streams
We are a love story and when I sleep I see the best
scenes

I think your loyalty has left me gifted
They call it falling in love bit I feel more lifted
Like you're part of me and helped my spirit
In a short time you've made me feel a way I never
knew existed

Together with lit candles you'll see the part of my
heart you came to be
That in my arms where you belong you can freely
breathe
That soulmates found each other and it's what I
believe
As my lips touch yours,chest to chest,we are but one
heartbeat

Page 3   "Meâ€¦.The Ghost"

In the silence of the darkness in the empty house I
wait
Waiting for you to come home
I sit on the couch watching the clock as I glance at
pictures of us from earlier dates
Oh how I hate being all alone

I've been here for awhile now
Trying to reach you
You walk in the doorâ€¦I open my arms to embrace
youâ€¦I wish you could feel me somehow
I pat your back as you cry,I know the death of me
emotionally beat you
I watch you with your new boyfriend,it hurts so bad
But I can't expect you to be alone

I wish I could apologize for the arguments we had

How I made it hard for our house to be a home
And now you can't see me but I'm here for you
I still love you
I try to wipe every tear from you

You stare at the sky,talking to me like I'm above
you
But I'm sitting here listening to you talk
I hear you tell your friends you miss me
I sometimes leave to go for a walk
And at night I put my lips to yours and remember how
you kissed me

I lay next to you at night when you need someone to
hold
I joke with you, you don't hear
But you said out of everyone I made you smile the
most
I hope to see you prosper,to never be hungry,or hurt
or cold
I promised you forever so I'll be here,just me,the
ghost

Page 4   "Find Me In The Stars"

Selfish will be my titleâ€¦the way I chose to leave
To fly away to the places I can be free
To the places only some believe
To a place I could always see

With my smile I gained friendship yet when in tears
they walked away
So sad my heart doesn't work that way
My heart waited in its own locked cageâ€¦
For someone to care enough to open it and let it see
the light of day

Tears and anger unaccepted,unwelcome,unwanted
As I lived for so long with my shell so haunted
So betrayed by those that made promises or those
that didn't love me enough to make a promise at all
Those that got so used to my smile they never
thought I could fall

All of us have monsters under the bedâ€¦in our head
They claw through some of us assuring every breath
means another breath closer to dead
Our story only seen for days as everything in life
moves on
Pictures and posts exist talking of how they can't
believe you're gone

But someday I know I will float away
To an existence out in space
To hug the milky way
To finally stop fighting a losing battleâ€¦ To stop
running an unwinnable race

They'll remember me they said they'll love me
forever
They'll keep my memory close although I'm far
And as they look at the sky together
Maybe they'll find me in the stars

Page 5   "The Doorway"

Enter knowing my broken soul
Be aware of the emptiness,the void where my heart
once was
Come into my existence to stare into the eyes of a
walking,shallow hole
Beware of the sadness,it doesn't want to show itself
but does

Enter my life with good intentions and believe in me
I've stepped in quicksand a slow sink to suffocation
Study the feeling of pain and tell me what you see
in me
My mask so rusted,my rage displayed with no
hesitation

Learn of my lack of patience and peace of mind
Give me a reason to see past the illusion
Sensitive sacrifices mixed with powerful regrets and
dissatisfied sighs
Be my reason to let go of the confusion

Knock at the door expecting a discontent answer
Spirit sucked into the black hole to a place beyond
my vision
So many different types of me,my mind,my cancer
My inability to be OK with a decision

Know all of this to be true
So appreciate and remember when I walked in the
doorway how much it took for me to smile at you

Page 6   "Guardian Angel"

There was a sound of a caw from a crow to the left
of me as thunder echoed from endless space
I felt tiny drops of rain begin to hit my face
I opened my umbrella to keep from getting wet
Surrounded by tombstones and sitting on yours as I
flick my cigarette
You were so specialâ€¦everybody saw it in
you,especially me
As I glance at your grave I hope in death you
finally got to see

You were too angry,too void of others worries
When you wanted something you wanted it in a hurry
You were hard to deal with we all worked hard to
understand you
How you got so shook up when plans fell through
I saw your tears,they came more often than you liked
Depression taught you a lesson but you put up a good
fight
You were a soldier in a way you were battling wars
inside
You never realized how your sadness also made me cry
You were surrounded by love and yet you never
witnessed it
You said you wanted to die and it hurt those that
wanted you to have life but couldn't give it
Your bad attitude had me on my toes
Your fights you thought you won I helped you win
those
And the love you lost was your fault you always
would push people away

You sometimes sometimes strayed from your dreams so
guided you along the way

As it began to pour a tear dropped off my cheek
I tried to save him but perhaps I was too weak
"I'll love you forever" I say then sigh
I spread my wings and fly high
As I look down one last time at your grave
I say "I tried to help you from every angleâ€¦
But it sure was hard being my guardian angel"

My head rested on the blankets as the stars shined
for me again
The waves of the ocean smashing against my feet
How could my mind still be on the pain as the tenth
falling star shoots toward its final destination
The smell rested in my nostrils reminding me of the
freedom I didn't have prior to my change
I turn my head to the left,a missing piece of my
life as no one was lying next to me
My left palm aching for someone under the same sky
just different clouds to accompany it
A single tear fell as my thoughts of my failures
punched the inside of my brain
A sip of my whiskey set my throat on fire igniting
my insides with wicked abandonment
As I set down the bottle to grasp and turn the lid
of my pill bottle open I think I forgot
I forgot what I was doing this forâ€¦.still
breathing
Pictures of everyone's smiles filled my head
We used to be so happy
I swallow a bunchâ€¦a lotâ€¦.probably too many
It doesn't much matter after I swallow more with
another chug from my bottle
My thoughts begin to whirlwind as more tears share a
place on my cheek
How could they all forget me I haven't forgotten
them I thought

I begin to float on my back onto the great wide open ocean still staring at every last twinkle the stars allowâ€¦.and I drift away
It occurs to me that I can no longer stay above water as the waves become more unmerciful
I whisper "I'm sorry"
And right before I fall underneath the water I see a falling star againâ€¦.did you see it too?

Page 8   "No More Tears"

The short life lived by those that believe it lasts forever
The pain felt by those that feel untouchable
The loneliness felt by those that stay together
The joy of clutching what was unclutchable

Such a contradiction life can be
Live it fast end it fast or live it unable to see
Such a twisted world behind those that swore they were free
Such a double edged sword called happiness or glee

Strangers become lovers to become strangers again
But it isn't how we see itâ€¦what we feel we know
That very stranger promised to stay til the end
But disappeared into the darkest part of our heart and soul

Tears fall more often as we learn
Smiles fade as we become less blind
So hopeful for what's to come but in turnâ€¦
So scared of the things we have to leave behind

We all get away from ourselves and become someone new
A new lessonâ€¦a new scar
We say we'll never change but that's what we do
Especially when those that seemed close grow farther apart

We all could use a helping hand in life

We all are certain to die
No one knows their personal price
But to walk away on your own is to know you still
might cry

Enjoy your time,your minutes,your years
Take ahold of your fears
And even when you feel it's your time to go
Just thinkâ€¦after that there's no more tears

Page 9   "Sunshine On My Face"

The day I found out I'd never again see your face
I uncontrollably wept in a cell
I apologized hoping you heard me from some unseen
place
My broken soul leaked as tears fell
My heart stopped, I swear a part of me died with you
My shattered spirit ached to my bones
Thoughts of all I took and the nothing I could give
you
I should've been with you,you shouldn't have been
alone
Guilt and shame haunted meâ€¦.still possess me
The joy you gave me is gone
I imagine your smile and you sitting next to me
I close my eyes and hear you sing your songs
There's a place in my heart where you're alive
You speak to me in my dreams
You will always survive
Your ears hear my silent screams
Your greatness I'll never achieve
Your spirit is in the air I taste
Deep down I believeâ€¦.
You are the sunshine on my face

Page 10   "Sunshine On My Face Pt.2"

I close my eyes and think of your face

With your smile illuminating my heart
I hope there's an afterlife and I'll see you in some
beautiful far away place
So I could finally thank you for being by my side
from the start
All that you sacrificed for me I took for
granted…this I know
I'm so regretful that I didn't cherish all my years
with you
I had the best person I'll ever meet next to me
filling me with her glow
And now you're gone there's nothing I could do
It's been three years come tomorrow since you left
I've called it my motivation…my inspiration…my
new start
But deep down to me it's a terrible loss…a
tragedy….a theft
Although you continue to glow as every day you show
up in my heart
This Christmas will be my first with a family of my
own
I sure wish you'd be here to see I got myself
together mom
I finally have a home
And I'm keeping myself out of trouble and free
You'll always live through me
You still are in the air I taste
And even though your physical being can no longer be
You'll always be the sunshine on my face

Page 11   "All That You Are"

Amongst the clouds,behind the storm,there you were
Drifting into my life like a feather in the wind
Drenched in rain we didn't think an end to the storm
could occur
We didn't think it was time for a new season to
begin

The once vanished sun peeked over the horizon
It lit up life before our eyes
The wind blowing hope into our hearts

The fresh flowers blooming to our surprise
It was time for a new beginning to start

In your eyesâ€¦.the warmth of a bright day
Melting the ice cold heart I had obtained
On your lips the sound of a spring day
I closed my eyes and listened feeling my dreams as
they were regained

Every so often the thunder of two energized souls
collides
Soon to be swept away by the sunshine of love
The fresh smell of grass sits by your side
And the beautiful sky is above

In my chest urgency,in yours the calm
Beating together in unison with a new way of life
The sound of waves and the sand under our feet is
great as we lay underneath the palm
The hand in hand with fate as our connection will
make us husband and wife

Feeling the magic of each other's touch as our minds
run away
To the paradise we make
Hearing the birds chirp as night becomes day
Knowing we'll never be alone if this world should
break

The sound of silence broken as I say I love you
While we rest our heads and smile looking at the
stars afar
Knowing I believe as you say I love you too
That fallen star a wish for someone else,for my wish
is all that you are

Page 12.   "Feel The Earth"

Such shallow souls we've become
Talking of ourselves... Living life as we wish
Almost robotic in our actions... Numb
Never taking time to appreciate our biggest gift

The beauty of dusk... Energizing dawn

When spoken of it falls on deaf ears
Through generations the loss of interest... The yawn
Although it's been our biggest supporter through the
years

While at the top of the mountain... The view
Such a wonderful display of what not to leave in
dismay
More beautiful than beauty...from the tallest
tree... To the morning dew
The oxygen filling us with life... The only place to
stay

Hear the waves crash down
Rub the water into our skin
Shine brighter than any crown
The sun... The moon... The universe grins

Fate... No mistake...an imperfect solution
All the geniuses that had been birthed
They lived with one resolution
They loved the stars...the air...they felt the earth

Page 13.   "The Peak"

From the bottom of this cliff looking up i felt
intimidated
It reminded me of the first day of school every year
Or when I was into someone...the first time we dated
But I had stopped moving...inertia...it was my wheel
to steer

By the time I was half way ascended I felt fear
Like the first day I was put into cuffs
My hands gripping onto sharp rock with no place to
put my foot...nothing near
But at this point there was no way I was going to
give up

As I approached the top I felt pleasure beyond
belief
As if my soul was being rubbed by soft hands

And I knew even with scraped up hands and knees this
was relief
Gotta crawl before you stand

I stood at the top of the cliff breathing in the air
I'm still lucky to have
A tear of joy drops from my face I wiped it away to
enjoy the view
In this moment...I had to laugh
This cliff was life...and from the top I yelled "I
love you"

Page 14.   "Blind "

Black was all that was left...no new sights for me
to see
Just darkness...no glimmers of light for hope to
show its face
I had been here before...I had been less free to be
With crucifixes as decorations and laws to keep me
in place

This dark existence allowed me to believe all the
negative predictions I would hear
And I could not be dedicated to the dream I had
envisioned
So therefore this darkness had developed fear
Living with it...worse than any torture or prison

In this darkness all I have left is my mind...my
thought process
And I let it bounce back and forth until I can't
stand what is still mine
Only after becoming nauseous
I could realize I was running out of time

And so one last time I thought of the sun moon and
stars
I dug deep into the truth I came to find
And I opened my eyes to a light from afar
And I open the eyes of others now...you only imagine
that you're blind

Page 15.   "Through Teary Eyes"

I do not expect you to stand next to me in this
world of despair
My own fortress of solitude where I stand alone
As I watch the willows drift others wishes into the
air
I think of my emotions of stone...the place I now
call home

My sickness has left me desolate and bare
My energy non existent my heart broken into shards
of regret
My moods and head hung low ignored amongst a caring
stare
Bipolar disorder...has me out of order...an
enigma...for there is nobody there

All they see is the heat... the flame I display
Inside deep the blizzard exists
And while I inspire with my exoskeletol ways
Inside hidden all the truth is

Oh what I would give to cry a happy tear
To mean all the good that I supply
But still in this deep void lies fear
And so I write and write hoping they
notice...through teary eyes

Page 16.   "Dreams"

For wolves there is no empathy
No pity no shame
For in a dream I saw sympathy
In a dream when I had a name
But time has no statue
Life has no direct guarantee
And you can be happy for those that have you
But who is happy to have me?
My sorrow has taken today and borrowed tomorrow
There will be no payback no return
In my dreams I smile without a feeling so hollow

Without a happiness I watched burn
Before I closed my eyes I thought of life...the
world...my size
I had seen that I was nothing
Heaven is not a prize
When I leave I have to leave behind something
In my dreams it seems I have a vision I'll never see
A cloud I'll never get past
A person I'll never be
But until the day my breath is my last
I'll fortify a dwelling in my soul
A place I've escaped the empty me
I can feel it close I've escaped my hole
I've been present in my dreams

Page 17.   "Shine Your Light"

I know at times this world could be cruel
Taking your kindness for a weakness while playing
you for a fool
For a fool is given shelter under anything they find
But the genius finds shelter in the mind
When it rains in your heart and you cry until you
can't anymore
Always keep at bay what exactly your living this
life for
For your purpose is your gift and your gift is your
purpose
We all have at least one and if you don't know
it...learn this
When your soul has gone ice cold...frigid as January
winter
Always keep beside you food for thought...dinner
For food for thought will spark your hunger and
hunger will spark food for thought
So eat well...remember everything that the starving
forgot
When the night is silent and you feel so alone
Look in the mirror and see the only thing that is
your own
For in the mirror is the smiles the tears the pain
the result of this fight
Open the door....shine your light

Page 18.   "The Empty Casket "

It's amazing how life works...I never appreciated
time until it was lost
I only valued money until I experienced how much a
missed day costs
I played with people's hearts until I had my heart
broken
And I couldn't pick who I wanted to be until I found
out that's something that can't be chosen

Drug use,wild crimes,and two suicide attempts
without ever thinking of my parents friends or sons
I believe it was fate that kept me from that bad
side of the gun...the tag on my toes
Unfortunately I can't say that about everyone
Because people have been buried that have done less
than I've done

Heroin has killed my community and some of my
friends
Either people are in need of drugs or behind bars
What changed me was seeing so many others end
And falling in love with the stars

I suppose you would have to be me to understand
To go through my pains...my incarceration...my hurt
But it had made me a better man
And all the bad kept me out of dirt

There are people I miss I can never stand next to or
surround myself with
Because they are dead or have drug addictions with
no want to get past it
My losses are my curse and my gift
That's why there's no obituary for me...just
time...opportunity...and an empty casket

Page 19.   "The Painting "

This was his only outlet his only escape

A stroke of a brush...the vision in his mind
All his emotions...nothing at all fake
A new painting was needed...it was time

For all the turmoil that burned in his soul until he
needed release
It felt like an empty canvas would be the only
way...a new vision
His only way to embrace peace
A reflection of the misery he was living

All the beauties of life have been unnoticed
And even the shades of his art became darker
He had become withdrawn and there was but few others
he spoke with
Life was just harder

And on his final day he finished one last work of
art
A picture of black...as he felt his soul fainting
This was all that was left in his heart
It showed...in the painting

Page 20.   "In The Eyes Of The Lost"

So sad the little children have a forced smile...a
mask of acceptance...
A hidden place for disappointment lingers in their
world
Thinking...not fully knowing...but trying to
understand
Why is their mommy or daddy on drugs?why are they in
jail?

Their tears seem less and less noticed as their
parent drifts away into addiction
The future of our country born into pain... raised
to pretend it isn't there
But someday they will be grown...and able to let out
the sorrow they've stored in their own personal hell
They will let their voice be released from their
silent cell

Recently prayers have increased
But to them the answers have been declined
So how long will it be until the prayers decrease
too?
So many broken children that are expected to grow
and lead humanity but they themselves haven't been
led

They shed so many invisible tears...
They want love like anyone else
Put down the drugs...stay away from crime...lead the
children in a fight against their fears
For they seem too familiar...I see myself when I
look in the eyes of the lost

Page 21.   "Of A Broken Heart"

In a world so cold...I faced the winds of change
The early deaths...the imprisonment...the altering
of my face...age
I had written my heart...spoke my soul...I had hoped
to keep a wondering brain
I had finished a poem only to read it over with a
bloody razorblade next to the page

I had been to rock bottom with a shovel in one
hand...a dream in the other
Refusing medication for my sadness
I had felt the pain of betrayal from my so called
friends,lovers,and brothers
When I look back it was a life filled with
disturbing madness

I had dreamed of standing on top of everest but
never trained
I had always wanted to travel but always stayed
I had potential to be wealthy and rich but never
gained
I had seen and heard of the obvious good choice but
my curiosity swayed

And now that my life is over I wished I would have
lived a different way

That I would've grabbed hold of the stars and
drifted away regardless of the dark
But now...as they lower my casket they have only one
thing unique of me to say
that I was the only man to die of a broken heart

Page 22.   "The Reflection"

I'm nobody special...though I have tried to be
Hoping what I write could touch another soul
But I fail...I've ran blindly into mediocrity
And presented a warm heart to a world so cold

My whispers into the ears of deaf lives...no one can
hear
No one can witness my invisible drive
For i have lost hope...and gained fear
And my fire is dimming...I have no energy to strive

For in the eyes of the lost...I had bowed my head in
shame
I had let them down
I had remembered faces and forgotten names
I had disappeared...only my words to be found

But most of all I hang my head in doubt
My dreams seeming bleak
The light I shined has been burnt out
All this death...this sadness...this being unable to
write has left me weak

The mountains I've hiked I had carved my name along
the way
I have left my burden...my fears...my weapon
And in the waters of life as they sway,
I have left nothing to anyone...but my reflection

Page 23.   "The Fighter"

It hurts me to know you will never see my face
And that we will never get the chance to bond
For i know your soul is in a different place

And the day you were born it was already gone
When you were in your mother's belly I saw you move
I saw your little heart beat
I told everyone you were strong like me
Now all I have is the prints of your tiny feet
And a dream that somehow someway one day we could
meet
With the complications I know you were giving your
all...
That you wanted to stay
When I spoke to you did you hear your daddy call?
Or were you dreaming...letting your mind drift away?
The breeze blowing through the trees sounds to me
like the waves
I wish you could hear...
That I could've heard a breath from you and held
your hand one day
But only in my heart could you be here
So I give you all the credit...in a world so cold
you put your little knuckles up to remain
And I cry at times that you hadn't made it...I guess
even the best of us get tired
But forever the world will know your name
And I'll tell everyone your legendary story...of my
son king...the fighter

Page 24.   "The Haunting"

I sit alone in this four cornered dark room...just
me and these ghosts
They call to me more often than I'd like
For i am the guest they are the host
My body their home and they claim they're the reason
I still fight...

They take my sleep...keep me weak...keep me
wondering what will happen next
Will I lose touch with who I am? Have I lost myself
already?
These specter hold me responsible keep me perplexed
And in return for all the days I've fed them...they
gain no weight...for only my shoulders get heavy

I've drifted like a message in a bottle to a place
lost under dark clouds
Like the blind I reach for my better me...
My eyes surrounded by flashing memories and days
that make me less proud
And slowly but surely they better me...just an sos
no one will see...help me

Torture my focus with pessimistic thoughts
They are more consistent than any person I know
It no longer matters...the time I still got
For all that matters is I let people see the
show...and while I perform I'll try to glow

Til I end these different beings or emotions or
spirits I have inside will show their face
Leaving me a disappointment...unloved...wanting
Hoping for a better time and place
A place where I no longer feel...the haunting

Page 25.   "The Pianist"

They clapped their hands once again for him...some
with tears in their eyes
He filled the theatre with joy
His fingertips his Orchestra his weapon his life
It had been that way since he was a boy

The beauty of his words without a tongue
The height he'd reached
The high notes he would hit without using his lungs
The pain the happiness the story he would teach

So many smiling faces because of his art
So many times he's closed his eyes and played to cry
The natural urge he displayed on keys from his heart
And no one...truly knows why

He was forced to do it to keep from the pain
When the curtains closed he would to his torture
vanish
His songs played not in vain

His release from all the anguish

He himself on a tightrope keeping him from death
His steps with no net
Yet every tune ended too soon
Just so he wouldn't end it all...the pianist

Page 26.   "Skeleton Key"

I've held onto this key for a long time now
in my pocket for safe keeping
Hoping I'd feel safe to give it to
someone...someday...somehow
But my days are longer and I'm older and the the
window is dim...too foggy to see

I know this key opens up all of me
It would allow our souls to mesh like waves on sand
It would allow you to reach into my lungs and help
me to breathe
It would let you enter my brain...to entertain my
pain...until it was gone away
With this key you could be the reason I become
aroused...the only reason
You could walk all the halls of my bruised up heart
and let it bleed...let it bleed love
You'd gain permission to swim in my ego fixing all
the bad wiring...the vain thoughts
You could control my smile...stretching out my joy
like a cloud stretches the sky
You could control what I need to be
controlled...tame the beast inside...fill me with
just the right amount of pride

But where are you?
I wake up and live my day and go to sleep just me
Dear companion reach out like it's the most
important thing you can do
Because ironically I feel like I'll be buried...just
me...and my Skeleton key

Page 27.   "Alive Again"

As I opened the door and stepped out into the air
I lived a thousand moments in one
The sky called my name with tenderness and care
I feel the strength...the power...the sun
Each cloud painted a portrait of my favorite face
The wind gushed just for me
The leaves floated off of the trees in a
Symphony...followed by a butterfly...everything in
place
My vision excelled...all of life for me to see
A silent buzz rang in my ear as if I was in flight
The grass swayed...a rhythmic dance
The birds chirped....the ants crawled...everything
so right
A rabbit hopped across the yard and gave me a glance
I breathed in the elements and gained intelligence
and clarity of thought
I have everything I need...the earth...my friend
Made me anxious for the moon stars and everything
the night brought
But satisfied and happy...I woke up...Alive again

Page 28.   "The Sickness"

I've tried to oppose this...my diagnosis
Inside my mind the darkest night and the brightest
sun...a day of jokes a night with a gun on my tongue
Moments when I have the courage to fight all my
fears
Hours later...broken with a pillow soaked in tears
They tell me to smile....it's like they tell me to
control the monster with ease
The happy moods have me stand tall...the others have
me on my knees
It's a beast an insanity and a way for me to reach
heights
So maniacal yet genius so wrong and so right
There's times I can entertain a room
Then others...filled with anxiety and gloom
The tornado gives way to the hurricane...all in my
brain...the pain

I believe it is a gift and a curse...for it causes
me to see things beyond normal perception
Then it takes a day away leaving me a disaster
waiting for another day of perfection
Bipolar disorder manic depressive compulsive
obsessive
Deprived of normal sight yet I feel as though the
other side of my brain is awake
It's moods help me write help me fight although my
energy it will take
A lit stick of dynamite...these four walls as my
witness
For I fear myself...it will one day kill me...the
sickness

Page 29.   "Dead Flowers"

The onlookers never see how long it took for me to
grow
The lack of everything i need...the hurt
For they see my beauty but don't ever know
That I began to hang my head low depending on the
earth

So deprived of the love and attention I desperately
craved
The need for the air the sun the rain
For my only joyful day the days I bathe
When the clouds show but never produce I wither in
pain

Standing tall to try to collect a thoughtful eye
Do you see me here...here for you?
I'm so much alive and don't want to die
Could you tilt me the right direction?could you give
me the elements to get through?

But sadly...unfed...unbathed...and ignored I've
decayed...shriveled into the dirt
The world wouldn't give me life...or power
They ignored me in full bloom they made my existence
worse

They had turned what was once beautiful...into
another of the dead flowers

Page 30.   "The Wind"

I inhale the beautiful breeze as i stretch out my
arms and open my hands to my sides
Pretending to have wings...
My mind so consumed in this moment
My imagination runs wild... I hear the voices of
those i lost in this gust of air
Speaking life to me... Speaking forgiveness for
letting go
For so long I've wondered why life was so hard...
And i had made myself... I had turned the tides on
the sea of trouble
Yet the freedom of this soothing swift punch from
the earth lets me know
It's ok...
I ponder time and time again about what happens
after
I study.... I feel
And although I've enjoyed the stars... The sea...
The sound of it all whistling into my spirit
I still want to know if the end is the end
It doesn't make me crazy... It makes me me...
A thinker... I'm deeper than every layer of the
clouds
And from a distance i hear trees shake... Leaves fly
I close my eyes... I step off the edge of the
cliff...
I may not fly in this life... But if there's another
then maybe then
It's a chance i took... The day i tried to drift...
In the wind

Page 31.   "Contents of.... "

This warm wet place sends shivers down my spine
Like a brisk autumn wind
Overlapping events that are not just mine

Like smiling by seeing someone grin... Seeing
someone win
This life flowing place still filled with pain
Like a womb... Like birth
This place created from memorable names
Like a memorial of hurt
No other place consisted of so many blooming flowers
Like a watered garden
This fortress has seen so many hours... Holds so
much power
After leaving an imprint on your face... Your heart
hardens
This so not known and rarely seen place exists upon
life and death
Upon the coming and going
It is brought forth by the flesh or by theft
A thoughtful mind could only see it showing
It is the residence of chaos yet the release of all
fears
It is the hello the goodbye the i haven't seen you
in years
It is the very place you escape to keep loved ones
near
This place this poem... Is the contents of my
tears.........

Page 32.   "Heroes"

My heroes don't wear capes they wore a fragile smile
They were very real and flawed and it showed
They'd fly into my life when i hadn't been hopeful
in awhile
They would omit a light in my heart forcing me to
glow
They would stretch the boundaries of friendship and
love
I believed they'd take any punch life could throw
They'd withstand any push... Resist any shove
They were invincible... I thought... But that's not
true... Now i know
Their fortress of solitude belongs in my soul
Where they can grow without existing to the eye
They could fight my battles and no one would know

They could stay there forever and we'll never say
goodbye...
They could leap over my walls in a single bound
Immortal inside me where i won't let them go
And i never thought I'd see them being buried in the
ground
I never thought I'd outlive my heroes

Page 33.   "Candlelight Illusion"

I saw you... Your shadow on the wall
As we embraced each other with passion
As the flame from the wick danced to make a moment
of it all
A romance some would now call old fashioned

I felt you... As you gave me yourself... As we made
love
As we exchanged heartbeats...
I shivered as my fingertips felt your soul as my
hands carressed everything above
Almost supernatural... Almost a science... A
chemistry... Our heat

I fell in love with you.. As the flames bounced
light off the wall into your eyes
Your perfume creating cravings in my senses
As you became my prize
As i let go of all defenses

I miss you... As the candle burns to it's last
flicker i stare... Theres no one there
And i feel confusion
As nothing is in my arms but air
.... Candlelight illusion

Page 34.   "The Mirror"

Hey you.... So life didnt turn out the way you
thought

You look at your arm at all those scars that you got
Only you know of those emotional wars that you
fought
And only you could wonder how when unmedicated you
made it stop

As i look at you i think of how your youthful mind
didn't think you'd ever age
How you felt so untouchable as your book turned page
to page
Those tired eyes used to be rare you never thought
they'd stay
But as i look at you it sure did turn out a
different way

I took a look at your damaged heart so eager in the
old days to love
Now so hesitant and stand offish when push comes to
shove
Only you saw the tears that came when it had been
broke
And only you know the air those you loved had
breathed into you... How you choked

You're aging with that comes wisdom... Less fear
Only you know now not everyone is meant to be near
Only you know how your mind body and heart has a new
wheel to steer
I know you well... I see you in the mirror

Page 35.   "The Love Of Your Life"

I saw the blank look on your face
The same face that used to light up my life
Now in your eyes i see distance... Youre in space
I'm still in front of you with the sadness cutting
apart my heart like a knife

I think of our talks our walks how i loved you so
much
How you couldnt love me the same
How i tried to be your crutch
But he was always in your heart your soul your brain

I have dreams of the good days with you when the
smiles were real
How we'd feel like we were meant to be
I hate him for the things you let him steal
And how you gave yourself to him instead of me

It hurts so bad... I still cry at times
I lost the one person i was proud to win
And as i keep you in this shattered heart of mine
Youre with him... The love of your life... Heroin

Page 36.   "The Lonely Lion"

Upon the open grass he sees his potential
His footsteps the sound of dominance,his tears
unseenâ€¦the king they call him
The great ruler of all he pursues
His moments of sadness never thought of
Only seen by a perception of powerâ€¦his weakness
his love,his pride
Protecting what's his knowing all that will attempt
to take it
His kingdom filled with the coldness in the wind
Hurting his vision,displeasing his sight
Tales of fiction told not to his face
The fear,the respect,yet the people wishing to lock
his cage
A showcase of pure power,a disappointment to him
Nothing to satisfy his needs,his wants,his reality
His age increasing and watching the rest move on
hurts
No one wonders of his feelings
No one thinks he is capable of feeling
His temper his distraction,his flaw
All his instincts nothing to anyone bit the
commercial eye
On his prairie he lays feeling so alone in the hunt
His mind his prison,his heart never to be questioned
His natural being avoided by the outlook of a
consequence
His judgment by others in the jungle

A quick way of knowing what is life and what is
opinion
He will take you out, he will let himself
grieveâ€¦.he will be killed he will die with the
belief
He is himâ€¦the lonely lionâ€¦.me

Page 37.   "The Slave"

In the dark pit waiting for a rescue
Beat up and battered from the careless hands of
others
The slave so hateful knowing he'll never forget you
Stabbed and bled by his masters and even his
brothers
Continuing to work as hard as he could for
loyaltyâ€¦for pride in himself
Hurting badly for being used for all he's good for
So many had seen him caged seen him in need of help
But in his dark room he paced waiting for the next
open door
Some had came and pretended to value what he had
inside
Some offered a trade for him for a higher price
But he became reclusive his only instinct was to
hide
For every time he trusted things didn't end up so
nice
His cries never heard no one ever paid attention
His whippings and torture left him scarred and in
need of a sudden change
And did I mention
That he is my heartâ€¦.the slave

Page 38.   "My War"

The quiet sounds of silence shoot their bullets
through my thoughts
The good,the bad,the ugly deaths in my mind of
versions of me

In need of a safe place in the desert in my soul not
knowing how much more I've got
They say we only live once but inside I've died more
than I let people see

Stepping through puddles of mud only trying to shut
up the negative perception
Inside the jungle I've built to give me shelter from
the rainâ€¦the pain
The backup isn't coming to give me heavier weapons
Will I die a victim of myself? Just a lone soldier
with dog tags bearing no name?

The whistle of shots flies by my emotions
There's no avoiding what's inside
It doesn't matter where I deploy myself,doesn't
matter what side of the ocean
There's nowhere for me to hide

Feeling solitary in a world I've made
Seeing one by one as good thoughts come and fade
It's all the result of a game I alone played
My war never ends

Page 39.   "Another Dead Poet"

I gave you my heart with the thoughts that I think
My soul poured out for you in my ink
So forgotten when not strumming the strings of your
mind
So lost when I was there for you to find

I lay at rest hoping I reached a part of you no one
could
I thrived knowing that if you could tell me you
would
How my words of sorrow and smiles created a
foundation for a tear or a smile
How we live not seeing not feeling just being was my
constant trial

Never made a fortune off giving you a way to accept
how you feel

Not once had I asked for anything but time to read
what I know was real
And to receive joy from touching you mentally felt
even better
But as I'm lowered into the ground my legacy will
live on forever

No one can take from me that which I immortalized on
paper
No one owes me not one single favor
My art will bring rewards beyond belief,all of my
admirers know it
You only become wealthy when you become another dead
poet

Page 40.   "The End"

We drift in the constant carousel
The sun energizing our being
The wars among the godly are the basic story to tell
As souls are left fleeing

The talk of right or wrong a discussion oblivious to
the obvious
We remain one
Yet ponder like a novice and worship the man behind
the gunsâ€¦the real devil
All beings from the sky
Proof not studied on a higher level
Not proof at allâ€¦for the right eyes
Hope for the afterlifeâ€¦.realistic dreams

A heaven and hell live inside
Our happiness our tears our fears
Created by the puppet master of the stars
Look above and know your belief is where you hide
But the end will never be far
Know the guaranteesâ€¦ Believe in what you may
And as the sun shines once more
Know your soulâ€¦.feel your day
There's a new day to explore

It's so much more than a broken heart…a take
friend
Let your insides feel warm and your skin feel light
again
As a supernova bends a black hole explodes
There's no way to pretend…we will all be blind to
experience the end

"The Dreamer"

Living life awake in a world of broken hope can ruin
your heart
So close your eyes and drift let your courage take
you to your favorite star
Don't listen to the words…listen to the world as
it speaks
It is there for a reason it is there to help you get
to your very own peak
The spirit of a lost soul will jade your crystal
clear path
It will leave you breathless and misguided it will
leave you flat
So grow wings of dedication and soar to the destiny
few have seen
Be in a place inside you many have never been
The storm of life will drown you in self doubt
It will leave you soaking at a doorstep cold hungry
and forgotten about
The loss of imagination ages you like drug use or
laziness
So see what only you see and gain a new perception
on all of this craziness
Before any of this can start you have to love your
reflection and even if you are your only believer
You know you can…you have to forever be the
dreamer

"My Heart"

You may not think you're beautiful or that you mean
alot to the world

But I'd be lost without my girl
I look at your smile and I realize every single time
that I've succeeded
That all the pain was worth itâ€¦oh how I love you I
hope you can see it
When the clouds disappear and the sun shines
I swear it reminds me of this love of mine
You are not my world you are my sun
Without you nothing shines and I become so cold and
numb
But you keep my heart alive and wellâ€¦safe from all
the sadness
You keep my mind wonderingâ€¦away from all the
madness
You are the best friend the lover the future wife
And in all honesty you make me strive for a better
life
Don't ever doubt yourself you're the reason I
haven't fallen apart
You are what drives meâ€¦you truly are my heart

"That Rainy Night"

I recall the night like it was recent though far and
long gone
I had been sitting on the porch in wonder of all
that had gone wrongâ€¦
The amount of ticks on the clock I had wasted up
until that very moment
I believe that was the day a new direction had been
chosen

I could no longer think the thoughts I had let
poison me anymore
I was always wondering why everytime I opened one
there was always another door
Friends had been whisked away in the wind
And I don't know what had me convinced, that by
waitingâ€¦.a new life would begin

I had heard thunder in the distanceâ€¦it reminded
me of how far away my good memories were

And the lightning before it made me recall faces and
names that now are just a blur
But the feeling of raindrops on my face made me feel
alive and well
The sound of the wind against the leaves made me
proud that I could stand up after all the times I
fell

Within just a few weeks I had looked down at the
fresh grass
I had forgotten about the dreary past
It reminded me of new lifeâ€¦and a word
automatically came from my throat
The only word to describe my lifeâ€¦.hope

"Dear God"

Youâ€¦you've sent the lights from the heavens for me
to studyâ€¦for me to know
And my gratefulness is something I possess but
barely show
Thank you for giving me the strength you have graced
upon my soul
The lion you instilled in me that roars wherever I
may goâ€¦
Thank you for letting me know I wasn't meant to fall
in lineâ€¦for I would never grow
Thank you for making me proud with so much charisma
because of you I am able to glow
I appreciate so much the way you've made it a
necessity for me to evolveâ€¦
Thank you so much for handling all the problems I
could never solve
I'm so thankful God that you have blessed me with
perfect sight to seeâ€¦
The senses you have created allow me to have the
perception of me
Before I go I have to apologize for all the lives I
ruined
I'm sorry for the parents I served drugs to taking
the food from their children's spoon
I thank you for taking the shame away for all the
mistakes I've made

And most of all I thank you God for creating this all and making it possible for my life to be made

"Holding Both Hands"

The man to my leftâ€¦sharply dressed in a suit that screamed successâ€¦he smiled a smile making me content and welcomed
He spoke into my ear assurance giving me confidence
He suggested I do what others wouldn't
And so I didâ€¦
I've known him since I was a child
He gave me energy he gave me rage
He stepped on the tail of the lion inside me
And while others don't seem to agree with himâ€¦I wouldn't be me if he wasn't there
He smoked his cigars and sat on his throneâ€¦he told me I was king
He told me I could have all I wanted and more
He's my friendâ€¦he's the devil beside me

The woman to my right â€¦
She's so beautiful and in a dress of white
She gives me encouragement when I feel like I want to give up
Her hug is nurturing and softâ€¦it is exactly what I need when my mind drifts off
She speaks with elegance and meaning
Making heavenly music play in my soul
I can count on herâ€¦she's trustworthy she's the personality we all seek
I haven't known her for very long
But since she's come around i feel light on my feet
I feel inspired in my heart
And at no given time will I hide
She's my driveâ€¦the angel by my side

Seeâ€¦.I'm not sure about what will become of all my
plans
Whether I'll one day break or forever take a stand
I don't know which one is better the woman or the
man
I've decided to walk through life holding both of
their hands

"I Understand"

If you hurt so bad inside and you feel I could never
understand that painâ€¦
That pain that consumes all your smiles and makes
you feel like anything that is good will changeâ€¦.
The pain that you can't hold back,the kind of misery
that makes you wish you would die
If you live with the agony of knowing your child
grew up without your guidance and you deserve his
hate
If you feel the despair and guilt of never being
able to know the real you and you know what is at
stake
If you have shed so many tears behind closed doors
it has become your fortress of gloom
If you live in each and every regret followed by
dark days no matter the sky or the room
If you wish you could just feel joy but the sorrow
haunts you like a ghost
If you find no hope no place to find comfort no
friend to stand by you when you need them the most
If your days are spent dreaming and you constantly
feel your reality is a nightmare
If you don't know your next move and know it will
all be forced by a life that is so unfair
If you have wanted to do nothing more than hold your
head high and make a stand
Trust me,believe me,and knowâ€¦I understand

"Eyes Wide Shut"

You had the ability to reach them from the farthest
roomâ€¦with words
To achieve an intimate connection with their
heartsâ€¦with what you had wrote
And now you search once again for yourself as it all
changesâ€¦you see them move forward as you move
backwards
With only a hint of the right words entering your
throatâ€¦
Is it a gift or a curse you've been given?
Only you feel the heartbreak of your self
disappointment
These scriptures of your thoughtsâ€¦your addiction
Your talentâ€¦decadent
You have grown so distantâ€¦maybe your words are no
longer worth their attention
Perhaps you and them can no longer relateâ€¦it could
be they're lost for you to never find
Maybe like autumn leaves your abilities came to fade
and breakâ€¦you don't have the words for that
extension
It hurtsâ€¦as you'd rather have broken hands than an
unsound mind
Just keep writingâ€¦if not for them then for
yourself
Hopefully you'll get out of this rut
And if you're talented enough a thoughtful mind will
pull your book from the shelf
They will feel your thoughtsâ€¦.even with eyes wide
shut

                       "Numb"

I've grown so fond of you
Wellâ€¦of the way you leave me feeling
I taste you on my lips and before I'm in any way
aware of it I once again experience my bond with you

This fuzzy emotion is it me falling into you? Or am
I healing?

I've tried so many and I know you're the one
You're my armor
You're also my loaded gun
My loverâ€¦my escapeâ€¦my abductor

Everytime I digest your love i become what every man
wants to beâ€¦made of steel
Unaware of every problem
Far from anything I can feel
The feeling I crave met as I feel you dissolving

All my demons lie underneath heavy cement
My head bowing to another tv show gone as another
has begun
My lovely pill on my tongue
Take me away, leave me fadeâ€¦give me the ability to
be numb

"First Family On The Moon"

When I was youngâ€¦.I'd pretend my dad would be home
on timeâ€¦or at all
Attached to my mother's leg with hope
That he would skip the bar and want to see my
faceâ€¦
That he would miss me
On nights that I had gotten so lucky I wasn't so
lucky
I had been so confused of his rageâ€¦of why my
mother would scream and cry
I would carry my bag of marbles and pretend they
were planets
I'd imagine being the only boy to know about
themâ€¦different worldsâ€¦my only world
He would give me moneyâ€¦to show me he was proud
I'd use that money to buy superman comicsâ€¦he was
what I wanted to beâ€¦he could fly away
I'd lay on my back porch and watch the night sky

The stars would help me tune out all the destruction
and beatings
My mother told me I could be anythingâ€¦That
anything could happen
Now looking back I was steering towards being
himâ€¦heartlessâ€¦a father with no valueâ€¦only
dollars
But after all my lost timeâ€¦and somewhere in my
lost mind
I still believe what my mother saidâ€¦and I hope
one day to forgive himâ€¦to forgive meâ€¦
And that one day if dreams come true we will smile
togetherâ€¦
We will be the first family on the moon

"Bloom"

I wanted to live in people's hearts for millions of
years like the brightest star in the sky
To shine when they stared at me
To give them a happy feeling in their souls when
they looked at me with their eyes
To give them all hope in what they see

I wanted to grow from the dirt like a beautiful
flower
To put smiles on the faces of those lonely and cold
That the thirst for water and shining of the sun
would give me power
To be a sight that would console

I wanted to be the seed that grew into a big Apple
tree
With me hanging from it waiting to see who would
pick me from the world I face
In the entire orchard they would see
I'm not the biggest or the more ripe apple but the
one with the best taste

I wanted all these things and now as I look at what
I've come to be
I see that I matter in each and every sky each and
every turn each and every room

I am wild I am free
I am in bloom

                    "A Day At The Beach"

As I lie on the sunniest beach I could find I stare
out at the water
It's so blue so clear so perfect
I look over at you
" I always told you I would bring you here.
I've missed you so much it's good we get to spend
some time together" I say.
And you just sit there so still so far away
I think of all our better days before you went away
"I'm not the same as I was when you leftâ€¦I've
become a better person" I claim.
Once again you remain silent.
"I'm so sorry for all the problems I caused
youâ€¦.I wish I could take it back " I say with
sadness mixed with sincerity.
You don't even so much as mumble a word in return
"I'm making all of myself now, you'd be proud if
you'd just knowâ€¦.I miss youâ€¦things aren't the
same without you by my sideâ€¦I'm glad we get to
share this moment next to each other"
And as expected you just sit there not respondent to
anything I say
So I turnâ€¦.you're the urn filled with my mother's
ashesâ€¦.I open you into the fresh ocean airâ€¦.and
you fly awayâ€¦.
"I always told you the first time you visit the
ocean it would be with meâ€¦.I'm sorry I didn't take
you while you still breathedâ€¦.but just as you
taught me to always be honestâ€¦."
I close your urn
"A promise is a promise"

                    "Blurry Faces"

It took me a long time to find out that most the
people you grow up with you won't die with
And that a majority of the people you laugh with
won't be the same ones you cry with

I had been warned that as I get older I would change
my way of thinking
My youthful mind wouldn't let me believe that
But now years later after all those long gone
seasons of breathing seeing and blinking
I realize my old ways are faded like an old tat

I've always had a photographic memory
I remember the names the words certain smiles and
moments
I held the people from my past inside of me and
rewatched them like a documentary
They stayed in my hidden compartments

I wonder of those I know nowâ€¦will they be there
when I'm old?
Will I once again change my circle and my commonly
visited places
Or will they just be another story to be told?
Just like my old friends I no longer recognizeâ€¦to
me they're just blurry faces

                    "Handle With Care"

"Hello,my name is joshua,and I'm an addictâ€¦." I
said at the most unusual na meeting ever.
It was time to tell my storyâ€¦at least it was in a
room full of souls that knew all too well what I
felt.

See I was born from a crack addicted mother, and a
father I barely knew at all.

I was deaf, I was underweight, I was a defect.
I had tried so hard as a young boy to fit inâ€¦but
it's hard when you talk funny and you can't hear.
I was called "skeletor" as well as the usual
"retard" and "crack baby"
But at the age of 13 I had found my first and only
true love.

Me and Melanie my best friend clicked like a seat
belt.
She understood me,didn't make fun of me and laughed
at all my jokes.
She herself was 16 and introduced me to a
needleâ€¦heroin
It took me away from all that I knew and all my pain
became its own

By my 20's I had been shooting dope so often I felt
like I had died and lived a new life a million
times.
Melanie was always by my side.
We'd only separate to do jail time or small stints
in rehab.
But even when I felt it was time for change it never
happened.

"And so now I'm here" I finished.
As I had died three months ago and spoke my story to
all those that had passed from addiction.
"Just for today" I added.
And as all the angels stood and clapped I could only
think of Melanie.

Unless Buddha is right life is only lived once.
We come,we go, we hope to leave a part of ourselves
behind.
And I didâ€¦Melanie is pregnant with my boy.
I hope he doesn't end up like me.speaking to souls
that will never have another chance.

But for those in the world that could hear me, don't
do drugs.
Don't cage yourself in.
Even if life isn't fairâ€¦.

Live it like it was meant to be lived…and if you
have a child….please….handle with care

"Monsters"

I closed my eyes hoping for a good night of sleep
Like a wolf I counted the sheep
But it always seems in these moments I think deep
About the things I should've let go or the thoughts
I wish I didn't have to keep

The times of my life were nothing anymore
Just seconds wasted on people eager to walk out the
door
Wealthy only in looks with values and morality so
poor
And it hurts I was so nieve to fall into the
footsteps of those with delusions of grandeur

Inside my head the past was so hard to disappear
from
The beatings my heart endured left me completely
numb
How easy it was for their misleading words to lead
me to succumb
And the pain I had experienced turned me into the
bitter man I had become

I guess I better watch my back from now on
And sleep like a baby knowing that the bad times are
gone
Still sad how I was influenced by all the wrong….
For my past isn't filled with memories…it's filled
with monsters

"Beautiful Insanity"

Even in those with the softest of hearts resides
madness
A wild untamed beast prepared for battle
Yearning to create carnage to all those that
disagree
I have felt this in me

Even among the people that have a brightly lit soul
lives sadness
A reclusive being with no home or friend
Searching for acceptance and love and never finding
the place or people to cause that to be
I have felt that in me

Even in the most optimistic person's brain sits
greed
A higher than thou parasite wanting nothing but more
Conniving it's plans to have more than anyone to
feel free
I have felt that in me

Even in the most settled of bodies lies lust
A sexual appetite unfed and in need
Looking for some deviant encounter while ready to
eat
I have felt that in me

All these things can cause a person to break
Hard hearted or not they are unbearable and more
than less felt in vain
But as I've accepted what I know is to come I keep
feelings alive and smile

Beautiful Insanity

                    "Paper Guns"

Don't ever let them tell you that you will fall to
your disease
That you are weak and living on your knees
That in your brain is a defect that will keep you
down forever

That you can't beat it because you just aren't that clever

Don't believe all the religious brochures you read
The ones that make you feel like you will burn eternally
The ones that say that just that one god sees
Live your life as you wish just place a few memories in people's hearts before you leave

Don't serve a country that doesn't fight for you
They make missiles while overcharging for food
We are "free" their approval is not needed
Open your eyesâ€¦live your chanceâ€¦absorb this worldâ€¦just see it

They don't want us having too many educated men and women
Their reign would be threatened then
So read write and stand up if not for you do it for your daughters and sons
It would be revolutionaryâ€¦for us to go from god fearing uneducated war seekersâ€¦.to paper guns

"Euphoria In Sanctuary"

I had to leaveâ€¦.to go to a place that made me feel
Because lately the people and life around meâ€¦it doesn't feel real
I wish I had another lifeâ€¦.but that's not something someone like me could steal
And so I wentâ€¦with my soulâ€¦the skin and my flesh peeled

I was deep in the forestâ€¦at a certain place I goâ€¦
An area where I just see meâ€¦a place I go when I no longer know
It was the perfect place to be when my smile no longer shows
And as I sat where I always sit the sun came from behind the clouds for me to feel its glow

From the trees the sun's rays bounced off a branch
and shined down below
It tongue kissed my soul
With a passion so intense I felt I was beginning to
grow
Not in a physical way but somewhere deep down below

The wind it sang a sweet song through the trees and
I once again felt love
My bones shivered to the powers from above
I fit in this world like a glove
I felt as though my wings had spread and I soared
like a dove

As the sun fell I stayed thereâ€¦I took a glance at
the stars
I felt them inside me as they are
It made me feel life and ignore any emotional scar
All my problems seemed so far

My fingertips made love with the world I knew I was
safe
The softness had calmed me down and this day and
night would not go to waste
And I stoodâ€¦.i stared once more at outer space
This was my euphoria my ecstasyâ€¦.my sanctuary

                    "The Day I Die"

On the day my soul leaves my shell and I disappear
like a snowflake in the sunâ€¦.

Cry no tears unless they are shed with happiness and
bliss
I myself have left a mark on hearts and there's
proof I once existed
No sadness should grip your mind or leave your lips
I was part of the bird you noticed in the sky,the
sea you listened to, the love you once resisted

Let every tear I spilled become an ocean for you to sail on
And every wish upon a dandelion I had thought up make your own
Every piece of paper I had wrote onâ€¦.
Like the tree it was let it be the reason you had grown

Look my children in the face and if you're honorable and humble take my place
Bow your head not for prayer but for silence for the sick and suffering
That twinkle from the star in outer spaceâ€¦.
Do not believe it's me just appreciate it while it's in your sight calming your warâ€¦.buffering

As they lower my shell into the ground speak of my downfalls
And picture a waterfall cascading down to the pond filled with beauty and life
The wind does not hold my whisperâ€¦a distant call
Hope for my return more than any afterlife

Keep our memories at bay to avoid any mental dilemma and take a step forward
Let not a life of purpose gone away be a reason to cry
I had my chance to shine and be your foundation
If you love meâ€¦build off me the day I die

"The Butterfly Effect"

I once told a boy he could change the world by smiling when not happyâ€¦.he did
As the evolving life around him changedâ€¦so did he
He was once a quiet shy kid
Stuck in his mind and waiting to break free
For the cocoon around him was not similar to a web
He wanted good and was taught good in the end
His wings only grew mentallyâ€¦in his head
For every soul he smiled at needed a friend
And so years passedâ€¦his smile remembered by the truly broken few

He entwined with fate like a wallflower's roots
And through his mistakes he grew
He became a well known respected human beingâ€¦a
tree with freshly hanging fruit
The day came so many miles and states away
One of those broken few sat with a gun to the
headâ€¦feeling like they had nothing left
And like a string becomes a shirtâ€¦a tree assists a
breathâ€¦.that person thought of him that one day
Lowered the gun and smiledâ€¦.the butterfly effect

"Hidden Treasures"

For the longest time she had wondered where her
husband was going.
He would wonder off for hoursâ€¦saying he just had
to think.
He would come back dirty and sweaty and after this
occurring so many times she came to the decision he
was cheating.
"So who is she?" She asked in anger.
"I have no idea what or who you meanâ€¦I'm just
doing something." He replied
"What is it you're doing?" She asked
"I can't tell you" he said with sincerity in his
voice.

Months later.â€¦she sat next to him as he lied in
the hospital bed.
In a tragic turn of events his health declined
quickly and he had but hours left to live if fate
was on his side at all.
He could barely speak but in his last conversation
with her he told her that when he dies she should go
into a box up in their bedroom closet.
Sadly he passed away an hour after that conversation
and she did what he asked.

Inside the box were 4 maps of what looked like the woods he had spent so much time in.
On top of the maps were the names of her and their childrenâ€¦.
So the next sunny day that came to be she distributed the maps to everyone and they went to the woods on an adventure to find the spot he had marked with an x.
After searching down by the creek for awhile one of them said I think this is the spot.
After looking at the map they decided it could be the spot and began to dig.

After about an hour their shovels hit what sounded like wood.
They dug it out completely to see it was a treasure chest.
Inside is what would make them smile or cry or maybe both.
There was souvenirsâ€¦stuffed animals and toys and there was an envelope holding inside a letter.
It read:

"Hey honeyâ€¦.hey kidsâ€¦if you're reading this then you made it longer than meâ€¦I'm writing this to let you all know that no matter the ups and downs struggles and hardships I always knew deep down I had the most special family a man could ever have. And i enjoyed every bit of it with you all. I hope that you all have the most wonderful life with the time you have left. I tried to be the best husband and father I could be. I made mistakes. I wish I could've done more for you all. Hopefully you feel satisfied with our relationship before I ended. I'll see you in heaven or in another lifeâ€¦.or maybe this is the final goodbyeâ€¦.just know and keep with you that I love you

more than anything….and thank
you for all the good times.…"

She closed the letter and with tears in their
eyes…they all hugged.
Even in death he brought his family together…they
became closer…and that is the hidden treasure from
which we all should seek.

"A Different World"

They always tell us to reach for the stars…
But what a different world it would be if we could
reach for each other.
We would no longer have to fear…the past…the
present…or the look of our scars
For we would be solid and never truly alone…we
would always have another

They say time heals all wounds….
But what a different world it would be if we
realized time doesn't exist.
We always focus on it right from the womb
Though without time yesterday never happened…and
each day we are reborn…it would help us to persist

They tell us to stay strong….
How different would the world be if they allowed us
to show we were weak…
If it wasn't frowned upon or looked at as wrong
It would help us to grow…to survive all the times
that were so bleak

They say home is where the heart is…

What a different world it would be if hearts were everywhere…worn on our sleeve
There would be no deceit…just honesty in all this
In a different world…I wouldn't look at the sky…and want so badly to leave….

"Emotion Bank"

I had felt like an emotional bank…my heart was the vault…and everyone wanted to make a withdrawal…I couldn't remember the last time someone left a deposit
My walls were cracked and vulnerable…able to crumble easily under pressure…leaving me open to intruders…robbed of all I stood for
My fragile existence standing on a foundation of loss and gain…in need of a clever joke…a forgiving smile…a brink of fondness
Instead….the crease on every dollar lie in a depth no one knows…my poor fuzzy soul buzzing surveillance…bearing witness to those still pursuing a dream
My illusion…a day where the inside of me shines…isn't filled with greed and pain…and heartbreak
I saw so many from behind my desk…with soft eyes…in need of a loan…in need of the same thing I needed
Disappointment lurks inside of me…surrounded by people like me…in need of a shoulder to lean on…only to attempt to rest their head on a phantom…cred
it that doesn't exist
But today just might be the day…that I close down..i am going to shut the vault before it's empty...i will forget the combination…and I the emotion bank…will remain air tight until I see a deposit…when I can get more than I give…

"The Evolving Lie"

I had broken so many promisesâ€¦.so many lies had
came from these lips
Feelings were hurt and I never felt a thing
She had loved me so muchâ€¦gave me trustâ€¦but every
untruth had the others eclipsed
I had kept having affairs and making her feel
worseâ€¦heartless to the tears I knew it would bring

My name is Matthew I am what the world would call a
player
Teresa is my girlfriend
Me and my friends joke and laughâ€¦they call me the
pussy slayer
Teresa found out about a few girls and told me
without me she would want her life to end

I guess in some way I loved herâ€¦but I didn't care
I enjoyed the sex the game and all that came with it
One time when her mom died she called but I was with
my side chick and acted as if I wasn't there
I wasn't ready to settle downâ€¦but I didn't want to
lose her either I admit

Just yesterday she caught me with one of her friends
She cried and screamed while I sat with a smirk on
my face
I would sweet talk her and she'd get back with me in
the end
I know she knows no one will love her besides
meâ€¦so no one can take my place

She cooked me dinner today and it filled me up so
much I had to take a nap
Life is good and I'll just keep her in line while I
schedule every girl that I see fit
Yet suddenly I just woke and my wrists are tied in
straps I looked at the edge of the bedâ€¦Teresa is
holding somethingâ€¦"Teresa what is that?"
She laughed "it's your dick"
I looked down at my bloody stumpâ€¦life is a bitch.

"Ugly"

One thing is for sureâ€¦.i always meant well
I've made the mistakes but deep down I always loved
you
Or maybe I'm wrongâ€¦there has to be a reason I put
you through this hell
I had you surrounded by large walls and confined to
your brainâ€¦sorry for the things I put you through

I filled you with false hopes and fed your
depression
With every disappointment I witnessed your willpower
break
I poured the gas into your soul and struck the match
to create your aggression
I gave you self confidence just to laugh in your
face and tell you it was fake

I held the razorblade as you opened your arms just
to feel
I palmed your skinâ€¦.
And as you cried I peeled
Pouring salt into your cuts with a demented grin

That heart of yours it was so warm so accepting I
had to put it into the coldest of places
I only wanted it to be you and me
And so all those people fell and slipped on your ice
cold heartâ€¦you felt guiltâ€¦I liked the look on
their faces...
When they realized just how deep I had dragged you
into a world they could never be

I'll get to your brain one day and I'll own every
bit of you
It's my version of love...I'll force you to love me
Because no matter what I'll be here no matter what
you do
Sincerelyâ€¦.bipolar disorderâ€¦by the way today you
look ugly

"The Perfect Storm"

Let me not walk alone…I need a hand through it all
For my legs get wobbly…and I need you to catch me
if I fall
This pushing down of my feelings has me stuffed with
self loathing soon I'll explode
Into particles of pain I become only for the broken
ozone to know

Let me not drive while drunk…I need someone to
help me steer
For I'm known to crash…I only survive when someone
that cares is near
This moving my way around obstacles I need to
overcome has me dizzy with doubt soon I'll collide
into my own low self confidence
Surely into a sea of self pity so muggy and dense

My shadow does not know itself very well
It comes and goes with no one to compel
And so what is a reflection of me disappears into
itself
Does that mean I never existed at All? Or am I but a
blue book on a blue shelf?

My fingertips sometimes feel good on my own skin
Does that mean they too can play the violin?
My shell has given me so many sad stories to tell
Still I betray every atom every molecule of
me…every cell

And so stepping both feet into my boat…knowing of
the disaster ahead…
Is it sad I don't care if I'm alive or dead?
I smile while I cry while I scream as we
interact…me and the biggest wave ever formed
I figured out the puzzle…here or gone…I've
survived the perfect storm

                          "Grandfather Clock"

Imagine….if your brain was split into two…and all the stars and planets were put in between…
Do you think when it was connected again you would see from a different view of life?
Would your perception reflect off the moon to create your own personal galaxy…your own scene
Would you still believe in Satan or Christ?
Wouldn't that make your thoughts the beginning and end of the universe…?

Just think…we are all the balloon let go outside…
Symbolic and free…
Drifting through storms and sunshine and anything the sky hides
But once we disappear who knows if they'll ever see us…or where we might be
Isn't that just like life…we show up to the parties we make people smile…but we get let go to vanish…deflate….lose what we have inside

Can you picture….we are the old shoes sitting in the garbage can
We've walked so many miles…hoping our insides would keep us thriving
But just like those shoes everyone knew from the time we were created we had a span
And now with holes in our souls…. There's no way to know how long we will be surviving
It's so factual isn't it? We get worn we fall apart and even our other half may come undone too…so keep your shoes tied tight

Close your eyes and think about it…think about being a child on the merry go round
It made you smile or it made you cry but it literally spun you through time
Isn't that all of us? Spinning on this planet…looking to feel that butterfly feeling in our stomach…something or someone to astound
Only to know it eventually stops…and we might not get another ride…

We are everything…we are but a tick from this big
grandfather clock

"Fingerprints"

I trust in the journey I've been released into
My bruised knuckles and bleeding heart mean nothing
at all
For i do not know when it's over… if I will have a
chance to anew
I'm only here to answer what I believe was my call

The tears of despair sink into you…or evaporate
into the air
Although you may not have done it all alone
After the delusion of time sets in…were those
tears even there?
They will no longer matter if there is a hell or
heaven we will one day call home

I just try to find the beauty in my pain…and the
bad side of happiness…a Zen like balance
I feel I search I learn and I write all the ups and
downs
One day the world will feel my absence
And I am sure to be buried in the ground

I've traveled many of miles with a blistered soul
It made no difference on the result or outcome of my
experience here
One day I will let go
And I will finally know the release of what most
fear

See I'm not timid to an epic change or a new breath
I seek them without being given a hint
The Day I come face to face with death
I know…in this lifetime…I have left my
fingerprints

"Wounded"

It's so hard to look at youâ€¦my baby boyâ€¦hooked
up to machines to help you breathe
I just wait for your hand to tighten in mineâ€¦so I
could know your soul is still alive
The heart monitor reminds me of the first time I
heard your heart beatâ€¦you being in my stomach made
me happier than you would believe
And nowâ€¦I just watch the lines and listen to the
beepâ€¦hoping you could find the strength to survive

I told you that those drugs would ruin your future
and destroy all of your plans
You were always so smart I remember how quick you
learned the abc's
I swore that you would grow to be a wonderful man
And nowâ€¦the doctors say your brain might not ever
workâ€¦still I'd like to think you can hear me

I look at your faceâ€¦I remember that smile and how
you always gave others joy
Now your facial expression is as if you're off in a
different dimensionâ€¦nowhere near here
You were beautifulâ€¦and you let the drugs cause you
to lose your wingsâ€¦you were more splendid than a
viceroy
And nowâ€¦I cryâ€¦I prayâ€¦I fear

I was asleep by your side when I heard the pitch of
the monitor go off
The doctors telling me there's nothing they could
have doneâ€¦
My heart was yoursâ€¦when you threw your life away
you threw our life awayâ€¦leaving me soft
And nowâ€¦I think of how wonderful you wereâ€¦and
how I'm so wounded

                         "On My Shoulders"

Give me your griefâ€¦

Your perception on painâ€¦long or brief
Lay onto me your discomfort and insignificance
Can I please feel your abhorrence

I have no thoughts of my own you are my master
You carve your undivided thoughts into this disaster
Cry of your negligence while lowering my importance
Feed me your doubt in accordance

Me I'm a sad counterpart to your laughter
I plee for you to not care for my heart thereafter
I am meaningless in a bit of devotion
My peace shouldn't existâ€¦cause a commotion

You are all that mattersâ€¦.you the ungrateful dream
If I save your lifeâ€¦.should I not be considered a
human being
Or should I die in your palms with an echo of my
cries in your memory
Your faithful accessory

I am nothing but a compounded soul
With strict regret in what I know
My thoughts wouldn't effect the warm or colder of
those exposed
Leave your existence on my shoulders

                         "The Falling Of Birds"

I can recallâ€¦.seeing an angel burnt to ashes and
put into a little pink box
It terrified me so muchâ€¦I never thought your smile
your whole being could end with this result
Not when I knew that for so long you were my rock
Creating in my soul so much tumult

There was always people who prophecized the end of
the world
I pictured a meteor crashing into us shaking us into
space
But for me it was the planet's loss of just one girl

The end of a part of my mindâ€¦.memories being the
last glimpse of your face

Your death made me feel as though the good people in
life would surely lose to the bad
That there was less hope for prosperity
My heart is still sad
At fate or God's true acts of barbarity

Hearing of you passing away was my ice ageâ€¦it was
somewhat of an apocalypse
It was the descending of the skies and demons
filled my life in herds
It was the eternal eclipse
It was the beginning of hellâ€¦the drowning of
innocenceâ€¦the falling of birds

"Wallflower"

Heâ€¦..being so unconfidentâ€¦so distant in his ways
Heâ€¦just wanted her to noticeâ€¦to acknowledge he
is there
Herâ€¦.so beautifulâ€¦so wanted by allâ€¦the one he
wants to amaze
Herâ€¦the one who has it all.â€¦the one who doesn't
care

Heâ€¦.has his back against the wall and just wishes
for someone to want him
Herâ€¦.turning others downâ€¦not good enough to
dance with her
Heâ€¦.has a worried faceâ€¦thinks he's not good
enoughâ€¦too ugly too slim
Herâ€¦.the life of the partyâ€¦.the one that's
noticed amongst the stir

Heâ€¦.never had a chance in his insecure mind
Heâ€¦won't ever live up to her standards
Heâ€¦.is friendly quiet and kind
Heâ€¦..has manners

She….will surely be successful
She….has boys at her knees that want a chance
She….thinks that all these boys are dreadful
She….walks over to he…."do you want to dance?"

"Metanoia"

I've dug a hole to the deepest part of my heart
In there I've found a want a need an uncontrollable
feeling of the need to stay in the dark
Pins pricked every millimeter on my back
And as I looked around I knew…I could never turn
back

A house filled with small rooms encompassed most of
my dwelling
Though the people who walked above caused it to
beat faster…become smaller…seconds of swelling
An insatiable urge overwhelmed each and every
butterfly that fluttered…invisible…but existing
I myself walked undaunted by the chaos…the
fulfillment insisting

Some rooms…glittery and filled with an
effervescent feeling
Others…filled with closets…dark corners….a
darkness concealing
Each step…a thought long gone had flashed into my
site…as if a blink
A hug I missed…a kiss I memorized…a welcome that
caused me to sink

This heart of mine had such a questionable past
A metamorphosis had begun…wings sprouted…my
torso a soul of distinguished fire…
No matter the seconds I could last….
I lived within my heart….i have felt the
rumble…I have witnessed the change….metanoia

"The Closed Mouth"

If Iâ€¦.drift away in the windâ€¦will I find a sea
to accompany my whims
A breeze to memorize my fragility
A road to curve my thoughts
A mountain to hold up my worries?

When iâ€¦.leave this world will I gather all my
comfort
Replay my life's role
Gain a pair of glasses that help me see my soul
Turn into cloth as I unfold?

Should iâ€¦..be a burden in my skin
Lay my head down if I win
Believe I'll pay a toll for my sins
Or be free as a dolphin as I swim?

Maybeâ€¦.i can sew a blanket of sympathy
I can gain the strength to share it with you and me
Cover my wounds as I bleed
Be a tall tree from an unnourished seed

Maybe youâ€¦.will hold me tight as I fall down
Lift me up as I drown
Ease my ears to the sound
The loud bang is all aroundâ€¦if I am lost can I be
found?

Do I knowâ€¦..there is peace as I grow old
Warmth as I grow cold
Truth to the story I've been told
An enigma I've been sold?

Is thereâ€¦.an opening in the out
A reason that I'm about
An answer that I'm without
Another closed mouth?

"Waking Organs"

It's amazing how you make me feel uncomfortably
comfortable
You shake the foundation of my heart
An earthquake in my soulâ€¦so adorable
No one could have thought this at the start

You leak some sort of chemical onto me
Saturating my life with your love
Evaporating into the air around meâ€¦making me feel
that you are there to be
Into the skies to bless the world even from above

Your kissâ€¦I taste something specialâ€¦I can taste
the stars
Sending me out into the galaxy
Having me float afar
With the air from you being transferred to me so
abruptly

Your skinâ€¦.soft as the feather of a dove
Each and every curve an adventure
Leaving me clueless to how you do thisâ€¦how you fit
me like a glove
My loveâ€¦my incredible venture

The feeling you give me is unmatched
No doubts live inside meâ€¦you the important
I feel so newâ€¦if you willâ€¦freshly hatched
Thank you for bringing me to lifeâ€¦waking organs

"From This View"

From this viewâ€¦.i can see you be all you ever
wanted to be
I reflect off the sea
Your eyes looking at me
And somehow I know that you know I've finally found
my peace

From here I can shine for you the way I always
wanted to

I can be admired for what I do
I will glow upon all I've loved…and lost…I can
stop from being blue
I speak from how I look…without words I coo

People believe in me
I am what they see
The look at me and hope to one day be as free
They can tell I am what they wish to one day be

I sit beside the largest light of the night
I make people feel romance and comfort on sight
I sometimes can transform a wrong moment into right
Because some people believe with me on their side
they'll win the fight

I miss you world…but since my body has died I have
become new
I am exactly what we're all made of…I am the star
you're staring at…I am also watching you
I shine in the twilight…I am part of the heavens
so many pursue
And I love you just the same…from this view

                    "One More Kiss Before We Die"

They say…love lasts forever…and compare lies to
staring at the sun
But maybe our love is a lie…foolishly taking a
close look at the sun…making us blind
For love should be a powerful smile…not another
eye staring down the barrel of a gun
It is a feather in the wind…free…yet
powerless…uncontrolled and not confined

When memories become the light of a dimming
world…questions arise in the heart
Questions that have no answer or reply
An awkward silence to a songbird sung start
A bowing of the last show…an unsaid goodbye

When the touch of another is numbingâ€¦and the butterflies have fluttered out of sight of your soul
The wild feeling has become a ghostâ€¦
The hand you held onto may have let go
That hand carries the parasite of infatuationâ€¦you were never it's host

The face that lit up your dark insides has vanished
And as we build up our belief to try
The person you found or found youâ€¦discovered the plan was for love to be banished
And neither will live that againâ€¦famine filled hungerâ€¦wanting one more kiss before we die

"Little Boy"

I woke as if in a dreamâ€¦I was walking up the street I grew up onâ€¦towards the house I grew up in I saw a little boy sitting on the porch with tears in his eyesâ€¦he looked familiarâ€¦I sat down next to him and we spokeâ€¦he had many troublesâ€¦I felt the need to speak to him of them allâ€¦so I looked over at him and I saidâ€¦.

Lifeâ€¦it's filled with so many different things.
There's loveâ€¦there's hateâ€¦there's peaceâ€¦there's warâ€¦but out of all of it you just have to find a way to be satisfied.
Friends will be loyal to you.â€¦friends will betray youâ€¦girls will love you with all their heartâ€¦and some will treat you as if you don't matterâ€¦but what matters most is that you treat them all the way you want to be treated. There will be successesâ€¦there will be disappointmentsâ€¦.there will be beautiful daysâ€¦there'll be days you wish you hadn't been bornâ€¦but most of all you have to move forward with your head held highâ€¦no matter what. If you get sadâ€¦if you feel ever that you can't take any more painâ€¦you shove your strength in pains face and make it wish it never messed with you. Be readyâ€¦changesâ€¦lossesâ€¦deaths will come

but the only thing you can be sure of is that you will never give up…do what you can to leave a legacy…a lasting impression on earth…be honorable respectable and loving…the world is already filled with too many of the others…and last but not least never ever follow the crowd…be yourself…many of the people you will meet will be clones…robots…nobodies…and that little boy is all you need to know

He promised me he would never give up
And right as I walked away from myself and into a big bright light I waved and thought…
I hope he has a really nice life

"Peace Of Mind"

I wish I could just find some peace living with this sickness
Killing me slowly with everyone I've ever met as its witnesses
I'm a cracked glass…leaking what makes me full…I will be empty and thrown away in time
A silent assassin of myself…the hourglass pours…a countdown until I no longer have my mind
People read what I've wrote and call it good…considering it as a success
But it's my brain in words…my thoughts…my stress only displayed in nouns and verbs
But I fear…what will happen when I run out of words?
I cry…more than they know…this disease binds me every second and won't let go
It's been winning lately…I fight still though
But it's bigger and stronger and I lose every battle going toe to toe
I fear they shall find me with a wound they cannot stitch or sew
And so in case time is short i joke I try not to let it show
I believe I'm made of a dead star and I won't let this clouded monster stop my glow

I was listening to Chris cornellâ€¦sad him taking
his life was not in any way good
But because of this warâ€¦.i deep down understood
I've become the dark store closed for years and
broken downâ€¦almost destructedâ€¦left a memory of
where I stood
Because I can't control a mood
This broken window a relief in the breeze
But unfixable and in darker winter nights I feel
myself freeze
Yet I look through the crackâ€¦wanting to be
outsideâ€¦freedom I believeâ€¦
Peace Of mindâ€¦is that what it takes for it to be
what I achieveâ€¦.?

"Counting Trees"

I guess I knew I'd end up here
In this straightjacketâ€¦to hold in my pain and
fears
To soak in my tears
To keep me captive and in my thoughts for the rest
of my years

(Laughter) they all love meâ€¦.i can tellâ€¦I can
feel
As my aura lights up this padded room like a rainbow
aside of dark clouds
I surge with energy (laughter) this feeling no one
can steal
A beautiful face stepping from the medicated shroud
(laughter)

2 hours laterâ€¦.

(Cries) they all hate meâ€¦a cannonball parachutes
this depression into my soul
Hitting the deepest of my hopesâ€¦shattering like a
mirror to lay in pieces at my feet
(Cries) they know I'm differentâ€¦they think I'm
uglyâ€¦they see me fall apart oftenâ€¦never whole

A dark black shadow moving around a lonely broken home…just bare walls and concrete

3 hours later….

(Growls) I hate them all…they forgot about me when I needed to be remembered
My fists clenched tight
A red vision moment…a peace murdered…to lay in a ditch dismembered
(Growls) rage filled my heart…the feeling there are many left to fight

4 hours later….

(Silence) I stare out this imaginary window at a long straight path…surrounded by trees…overlooked by a starry night
Looking at the stars…they've always loved me…they were always pleased
I belong in this sky…it's what has felt right
I smile I dance inside…I die counting those stars and trees

"Railroad Tracks"

Step by step…I walk on these tracks…making progress slowly but surely
The beautiful temperature slips from time to time
I had to move forward regardless of the love I felt so purely
The up and down memories I keep imprisoned in my mind

I leave ghosts of your faces….smiling…my old friends
The sky differs in time but my sorrow it stays the same
I could think of moments…I thought we would never end
But you stayed in the same place…kept rolling the dice…me I abandoned the whole game

I couldn't see any more sad facesâ€¦I couldn't feel
any more unbearable departures
So it's me hoping those I left behind catch up to me
While those that stayed have targets but remain
blind archers
In their mind they could reach itâ€¦but won't do
itâ€¦because they can't see

I fall sometimesâ€¦I get hurt
I look for company here
But I doubt my own worth
Throughout all the fear that exists I still move
straight I never veer

Yet the things we've done make me want to turn back
At the the same time I have to survive
I see us as I stare back
But some of you are no longer alive

It seems sad I don't have anyone but phantoms by my
side
And I'm so alone just to state a fact
I keep moving while you stay behind and hide
But one day I'll be where I'll need to beâ€¦waiting
for youâ€¦on these railroad tracks

"Butterfly In A Jar"

My eyes set on your colors
You display a natural beauty to all who look...and
to those who understand what you are
The wings you behold give sign to a picturesque new
day
So sad to see such an amazing creature contained by
self doubt
The holes poked into the top of this vessel of yours
still leave your life span shortening
My heart stares at you yearning to see you be free

Your inability to see your amazing beauty holds your
wing span tight to your body…hides all you are
My eyes grow teary thinking of your own self
imprisonment
You worry…you don't smile enough…you don't hold
your head high enough…
I am concerned…all the times I took the lid off
the jar…and you cower at the bottom…refusing to
come out
One day I believe you'll see what's your true
reflection as you look at me watching
Let the universe witness you pushing the top off all
on your own
You'll spread your wings so wide and let the world
know you're ready
You are so much more than you've given yourself time
to exhibit
From the cocoon of earlier days…to the amazing
woman you are now
My love…let yourself be…you don't have to
forever be….a butterfly in a jar

"Heaven"

Wait for me there….so far in the air
In that room behind the moon…where the weather is
always fair
Where the soothing music from the violin is played
on an instrument made of rare wood and spider thread
Where there's platinum pillars,diamond spiral
staircases,and lions laying next to my bed

At the big marble gates make sure it's open for me
So the walls made of Windows can open for me to see
and smell the sea
And my mind can feel young and free
So I can stand holding the loved ones I had missed
hands…and feel relief…and finally breathe

My thoughtsâ€¦as pure as the waterfalls I swim
beneath
My bodyâ€¦.healed and perfect beyond what I could
conceive
My ageâ€¦.forever young and soft as the sand beneath
my feet
The airâ€¦a scent of stars and lilacs in every
breath I breathe

As I smile without hesitation, I think of how I
waited my whole life for this.
And as I eat fresh fruit and sip my drink I'm glad
that I've finally seen my very own end
After deathâ€¦life's goodbye kiss
I can be peaceful now in heaven

                    "Astrophile"

I remember the day I fell in loveâ€¦oddly it was the
same day my heart broke
I was fresh off of a prison phoneâ€¦crying
loudlyâ€¦until I couldn't breatheâ€¦until I choke
I looked out the window creating a pool of tears on
the sill as my tears continued to spill
With a mind of pain,agony, denial, and it seemed
time was standing still
I looked up with blurry vision and saw the sun
shining on my face
It seemed as though it was shining directly at
meâ€¦into this cellâ€¦this small place
It made me feel alive and warm even in this horrible
moment I felt reassured
When I needed someoneâ€¦ I looked to the sunâ€¦and
it's love poured

I can recall moments when I sat with my own death on
my mind
Because of my sickness or because I kept hold of
some memory I didn't want to leave behind
Even on the coldest of nights I would look up to the
moon

With fresh cuts on my wrist it somehow loved me…it
told me things would get better soon
It lit up the darkest of my evenings it pushed me to
another day
By being the centerpiece in the galaxies masterpiece
it spoke thoughts of a better way
And so it nurtured me as I sleep
Watching over my dreams…and giving me it's
resilience while in holes so deep

I know I had lay and flirted with the stars so many
times
Never once did I leave with a bored or unhappy mind
I had shed tears of joy gazing at the constellations
and calling out what was mine
I wore the stars with pride…always inside…the
lion
I felt for me they shined….opening my eyes when
blind
Guiding me to know what was ahead and what I should
leave behind
They helped me recover…they showed me beauty even
in a world of ugliness I shook hands with life for
us to reconcile
Now I look to the skies…I smile…I'm loved and I
love back…astrophile

"Midnight Picnic"

Under this night sky we sit…me and two people
that changed my life.
With the blanket spread out in this long wide open
field of grass we admire the stars.
Together we enjoy the quiet,the silence of the
night.
And even in the dark I could see both sets of eyes
looking afar

I look to my right "you know you are the reason I'm
still alive right?"
She looks over at me " I think you would've made it
anyway"

I shake my head "I was out for the count….ready to give up the fight…"
She smiles at me as I say " But you helped me feel like I matter on this earth that day"

I look to my left "You know that you're the strongest person I've ever met right?"
She looks over at me " thanks but I was weak"
I shake my head "that's not what I know…when I looked up to you there was no weakness in sight"
She looks teary eyed as I say " if it wasn't for you I'd want death…whether an afterlife or eternal sleep"

I put my arms around both of them and the silence once again made it's way into our little picnic
" I'm just glad I could have you both here with me again" I said
In seconds…like water through the creases of my fingers and sand through my hands they disappeared…my stomach felt sick
At midnight that night I realized…it was my mother and my friend carissa…both still with me…both still dead

"Fade Away"

A woman came to me in my dreams.…she told me death is filled with loneliness
I awoke in tears…I looked at the scars on my arm,felt the hurt in my heart and thought…life is lonely too.
And so I went outside…I picked up a brown dry autumn leaf and held it in my palm.
I closed my hand and it crushed into a million pieces. I opened my hand to watch it blow away in the wind never to be seen again…isn't that leaf the same as the woman in my dreams?

On a day close to this one…I had been daydreaming…in deep thought about the leaf.

I found myself looking in the mirror at my changing
face and the gray hairs I found in my beard.
Time is just days and nights gone byâ€¦
But deep down I felt disappointmentâ€¦how long will
it be until I go by like a day and night?

I had a flowerâ€¦planted and nurtured by me and my
son.
But life around it had changed.
And just as it evolved by blooming under the
sunâ€¦it withered unable to fight the test of
timeâ€¦the cold world.
It saddened me, I am withering, i am shriveling up
and becoming a dead flower.

Weeks later during a late night, I thought about
that leaf and that woman and for some reason I found
myself in front of a mirror once again.
I stared in my eyesâ€¦they are slowly growing old.
The Beginning of wrinkles to show days and nights
will change me.
I wonder when fate will close it's hand,crushing me
to pieces until I blow away in the wind and fade
away.

"The Goodbye Cry"

I cried my tears into a cup until it was full.
And I sipped them with a caring heart
The tug of war inside of me was at it's final pull
And the core of it all tore apart

The hairs on the back of my neck stood at attention
like soft hidden soldiers
And my focus was the sniper of my soul
My fingers weak, being forced with the power of
boulders
Onto the trigger they pressedâ€¦aiming at a black
hole

My stomach turned like waves crashing inside

And my village flooded with pain
A paragon of swimmers still to die
The beautiful drowning of a name

A harsh embrace clinged to my thoughts
Filled me with an uncomfortable love
Although I was not for saleâ€¦somehow that day I was
bought
Into a new slaveryâ€¦shoved

A hurricane in my breath
Killing a world in one final sigh
For I do not want death
So I paid a dreadful homage to the old meâ€¦ with a
goodbye cry

                          "The Immortal"

This is a true storyâ€¦.

I was 12 years old writing my first poem
Sitting with fresh razorblade cuts on my wrist
behind a closed door in my parents home
I told my mother to tell my friends I wasn't there
as they called me on the phone
I bled out all the pain this mental sickness was
giving meâ€¦I needed to be alone

My poem was about living forever all the while I had
my own death on my mind
The blood on the paper meant something to those that
hadn't been so kind
It was my oath to myselfâ€¦the chemical imbalance
left me with not much of myself to find
No one knew of my emotional tortureâ€¦to the world I
was fine

In it I had saidâ€¦"to live is pain, to die is
retreat"
"The purpose is for you to build a name, a structure
of the memories never forgotten in defeat"
"Give me your brain, let you walk in the shoes on my
feet"

"Stay sane,wait for you and fate to meet"

I've always remembered that quote from myself
It seems me and my depression have outlived ages of
good health
I believe that's why,now, I no longer think my
number one priority is wealth
I make my name with no one looking…in stealth

My shadows shade my brain and I share no sorrow
I love those that make me smile at the thought of
another tomorrow
And even though one day i will retreat,I will pass
with honor and of high morals
Without a word being said,and all the blood I've
shed, I will forever be the immortal

                                        "Fly"

On top of the building he perched looking down at
the same familiar buildings.
Watching his family, his friends, and all the other
crows living life…ignoring his feelings.
His broken wing has kept him grounded for so long he
forgets what it feels like to fly free…
His only hope is to jump, to jump just to see…

His fear had him hesitant and confused as to what he
should do
What if he could no longer fly? What if jumping
meant his life was through…?
If he built up the courage and made the jump would
he fall to his death?
Would he smash into the hard concrete and feel his
last breath?

Then one day…he decided it was time
He hadn't experienced life the way he wanted
to…and so now he made up his mind…
He leaned over the ledge of the tall building
looking down at it all
And he kept leaning until finally he began to fall

During his descent like a gift from an unseen giver
his broken wing began to work
And he flew, he flew with more freedom than he had
ever flown with before
And as he soared and all the other crows saw a smile
on his faceâ€¦
He flew right to heavenâ€¦proof it's never too late

                         "Beneath The Oak"

Even though we've met in this lifetime I believe our
souls met lifetimes ago
Perhaps we were childhood friends in some other
existence
Maybe we held hands and were each other's first
kiss
Maybe we shared candy and secrets and pains before
all this technology or cars came to exist

Perhaps I picked you sunflowers and we smiled in a
world with less worries
And you punched my arm when I told a joke
In some other time I think we'd skip through the
woods with hopes and dreams in our minds
Hundreds or thousands of years ago I think you were
still mine

I wonder if on the very first ferris wheel we got
stuck at the top together.
If we were the first souls to experience that.
If I looked deep in your eyes
And kissed you until we were so out of breath we had
to sigh

I think we took walks to marvel at the stars
And we wondered what was out there together
When our souls were created and bonded as one
I think I enjoyed your company thenâ€¦under the moon
or under the sun

I have a deep belief that we lived a life of romance
and intimacy

Way before we've breathed even one breath in this
life
As the campfire lit up the night and the air filled
with smoke
Somewhere someplace j.k. loves a.g. is carved
beneath the oak

"Fireflies"

For those that feel aloneâ€¦.the captain's of their
own lonely boatsâ€¦
Sailing the sea of despair with only rain of tears
and waves of sorrow to surround
Lost In The dark forgetting the sun would ever rise
againâ€¦.
I want to be the lighthouseâ€¦.shining so bright you
can see there's a way back to solid ground

For those drifting in the wind like a dandelion
fresh off of a blown wish
Not knowing your destiny the same as the air from
the person who sent you on your ways lips
I hope you land in the hands of someone who will
make that wish come true
To give you purpose and to help them see to
believeâ€¦to help them get through

For those walking a road of self hatred and doubt
In the darkâ€¦giving up on putting their thumb
outâ€¦feeling forgotten about
I hope you see headlights in the distance
The one to save you and give you the ride to where
you know you mattered that instance

We all need a bit of light to shine
A soul or two to make us feel fine
Imagine how we look to those from the sky
The world is dimâ€¦.temporarily lit by the shining
of us â€¦the fireflies

"Save You"

I knew youâ€¦.our whole life we've been friends
You began to separate from meâ€¦I didn't know if
we'd see each other again
On your way you had a snake bite into your skin
And found your own hell inside of heaven

I hadn't seen you in awhile and finally saw you the
other day
With the snake obviously coiled around you lost in
your ways
With vultures circling around you waiting for you to
decay
Your obsession with the love of a feeling had become
a love that made you it's prey

We haven't spoke in awhile and I don't know why
I've tried to get in touch with you but you never
reply
The Last time I saw youâ€¦you had something hidden
behind your eyes
Perhaps the snake had almost fully devoured you and
I caught a glimpse of your demise

I came to visit you today and all I found was your
lifeless body on the floor
Not even looking like you with a wide open door
I cried because when I looked at you all I saw was
the snake
Just waiting for another person to pick it up and
make that mistake

I think you knew the snake would take you over and
betray you
That your life meant nothing to it as it would
slowly fade you
I miss who you were and I guess that didn't phase
you
I just had to look onâ€¦to waitâ€¦to hope that you
would save you

                    "Die With The Dream"

As you feast upon the starsâ€¦digest your fate
Grow your silver wings and fly to a place never seen
Use your hands to put the cotton candy clouds on
your plate
And if it rainsâ€¦drink it until you are clean

Turn the sun's rays to vines and climb
Feel the warmth in your bones,in your home
Throw a net onto the sun and bring it down to give
to the dark minds
And if it burnsâ€¦.burn alive but not alone

Walk on the waters of the sea and with your
fingertips capture the breeze
Keep the wind in your grasp
Fill the lungs of the dead that you wish to see
breathe
Even if that breath is your last

Surf the nebulas like waves and wave at the moon
Bring a tidal wave of constellations back for those
with hard hearts to see
Be a fallen star for those staring out the windows
of their room
And if they won't believe send a wish for me

When asked what people wantâ€¦they no longer ask for
world peace
Because like all of these there's no hope for it it
seems
But I still glow enough to imagine this at least
And if it is all truly impossibleâ€¦I'll die with
the dream

"Tears Behind
Shades"

We have the same faceâ€¦brothers it seems
Identical to some but not to me
I watched you abuse and neglect and ignore all that
have loved you

Your personalityâ€¦mister high and mightyâ€¦nothing
above you
Your first child was raised by another man
You were too busy to lend him a hand
You were so selfish and heartless I can't believe I
look just like you
In bathrooms we stood face to face I wanted to fight
you
But I could never leave your side,one day you would
need me
I can only hope you'd care at all to feed meâ€¦you
continued to bleed me
I tried to hold you back when you lost your temper
on so many people
I hated you so muchâ€¦you made me look evil
Your greed grew and deep down I knew
There was something I had to do
And so one day as you stood on a corner looking for
street fame,destroying lives with your drug "game"
I walked up close behind and yelled your name
You turned around and saw your face and I lifted the
gun to your head from point blank range
The blood from the gunshot turned your white
handkerchief red
The look in your eyesâ€¦long gone and dead
I wore sunglasses so you couldn't see my eyes
And I swear I saw our mothers tears turn to smiles
in the gunsmoke as it twirled and faded into the
starry sky
You never got to see my criesâ€¦for I killed all of
my own past days
No you'll never seeâ€¦my tears behind shades

"Otherworldly"

Loveâ€¦.love seems to be so otherworldly nowadays
For I asked my brothers and sisters for love and
they turned the other way
In my time of need they didn't have anything to say

And then they wonder why I look to the sky for it
all each and every day

We live on such a lonesome planetâ€¦a world of
selfishness and deceit
For I was promised so many promises that my friends
didn't keep
So now when trust is broken and the lies are skin
deep
Everyone questions who is the wolf and who is the
sheep?

Kindnessâ€¦.kindness is a weakness in this life we
all live
Hands are out for favorsâ€¦and there are some
willing to give
But the givers are looked at as outlets while the
takers forget their gift
I shake my head in embarrassment and I can't believe
how all this is

Loveâ€¦.love seems to reside in the sun moon and
stars anymore
For a person without a home is welcomed with closed
doors
It saddens me that there's not an open ear in this
lifeâ€¦this adventure we explore
The only love I get is otherworldlyâ€¦I don't want
to be here anymore

                        "Remember Me"

I hold you in my handsâ€¦my beautiful dove
You're the last beautiful thing left for me
I've saw your eyes wonder to the skies above
In this world there's so much to see

I have lost myself againâ€¦and again
My sadness anchors my hopes and dreams
And you stay here in my handsâ€¦.my faithful friend
I'm so grateful to have met you and shared my words
as we sat underneath the sun's beams

You have given me so much…more than I have to give
I don't think it's fair
You were injured when I first grasped you…but now
you have a chance to live
And so I look down at you…a tear falls from my
eyes as I stare

I raise my hands up into the air
I watch with joy and sadness battling in my heart as
you fly free
I can no longer hold you back…there's a place
waiting for you with great people there
And as you carve our memories in the clouds don't
look back…just remember me

"The Empty
Hourglass"

I sit back and watch the hourglass of my life
Each moment an ironic mistake
My thoughts magnify each grain of sand into a
reality of gone days and nights
Let me explain

In the first grains of sand I saw my sadness
How throughout my youth my lost soul held hands with
every dark cloud to pass
The inventor of my very own madness
And the destructor of all the good times that came
and gone so fast

Next as the sand fell through I witnessed my talent
and gift
How a paper and pen were my fountain of youth…my
Atlantis
Some would dream to put together what I've put
together as I've lived
Hence the bigger version of this

As the hourglass was half full I pictured a youth
wasted

Possibly I was considered a paraplegic as I had my
dream in vision but never did I chase it
Half of my existence gone so soon and forgotten so
fast
I shake my head as more of it falls inside the glass

I watch longer and longer as the sand falls to the
bottom
And just then it occurred to me…I had spent so
much time watching the hourglass I forgot about the
hour gone past
The past is the past and it won't change no matter
what I fathom
For all this time is borrowed…life is an empty
hourglass

"Dancing Silhouettes"

I look you into your eyes as we lock onto each other
The stars above twinkle just for us
No words are exchanged we look up at the moon at the
same time
The fire from the pit is in full blaze and the wind
is just fine

We distanced ourselves from the others at the party
This moment will send us on a course of blind
opportunities
And we don't know if we'll even wake come sunlight
It's a photographic second in our lives…this
setting…this feeling…you and me

Laughter from our friends in the distance reminds us
to smile
On this night…we love…we feel…
We mark our names into each other's hearts
This may be the only thing in life that feels real

The night so peaceful…so quiet…our hearts
beating fast
This is it
Time to coincide with this night we'll never forget

From the distance…a fire…a starry night…two
dancing silhouettes

                    "White Roses(A Letter To
                    You)"

I've fallen inside…so in reading this make a wish.
My dreams have hit a brick wall…my mind closed
into a disappearing box.
I like to believe in some other universe the box
appeared and I wrote legendary life changing poetry.
As for my current existence…just robotic
days…financial difficulties…a loss of
words…and an awkward feeling I've changed my path
without knowing. I laugh to myself
sometimes…asking myself questions…the answers? I
cry to myself sometimes. A tear on the ready and a
smile to act as a net…anything you catch I hope
you devour….food for thought.

I walk a thin line…no one knows why. Not me not
you. I just know the pain that creeps inside me like
fog to an already dark place. The only result…a
crashing soul…a road of demise…my vicious cycle.
You…you have breathed a breath to clear the fog.
By caring about what I write…even if it's a
temporary euphoria you send me to by loving my
thoughts I must admit I try to dwell there…in a
hammock by the ocean…until the skies turn dark
again and the waves wrestle loudly…too loud in my
head. Again.

I've been filled with doubt…a knife called
hope….jabbing myself until I pour all I have
out…but when I'm empty…another
circumstance…another negative bully to fill me up
and another sad day to sew me back up….a neon sign
flashing 'needs fixing' stapled to my spirit…and I
know the electricity will soon cause the bulbs to
die…so no one sees. So it's just me once again in
a dark room with wild fantasies of the day I feel I
matter again.

Maybe I was born into the wrong soulâ€¦ages ago I'd
be a kahlil gibranâ€¦an Edgar Allen Poeâ€¦this
lifeâ€¦a piece of coalâ€¦under pressureâ€¦but never
sure to become a diamondâ€¦a brief shine if
anyâ€¦butâ€¦in closingâ€¦.i have to thank you all
for reading what I've writrenâ€¦for taking the
timeâ€¦and whether I live another 50 years or
hoursâ€¦.i have become prepared to show my token of
gratitudeâ€¦ to all that have given me their timeâ€¦
I'll appreciate it foreverâ€¦for on the day I pass
awayâ€¦you'll receiveâ€¦.white roses

"The Eternal Night"

I have no vision but I see it all
With my eyes aiming at the sky waiting for stars to
fall
A blank look on my faceâ€¦a nothing wanting to be
somethingâ€¦so small
But with hopeâ€¦with hope I grow tall

Long gone people haunt this very night
With my mind holding onto memories of faces that
will never again be in my sight
But with hope I can reach higher than a kite can
flyâ€¦I try to grasp the stars...i might
Gravity killing my dreamsâ€¦but I hope stillâ€¦I
fight

I see my smiles within the beams of moonlight and I
imagine I have fallen into a black hole
That I'm not hereâ€¦maybe my shell is but not my
mind or heart or soul
And so I envision being in a place no one knows
A place I could hideâ€¦with constellations at my
sideâ€¦where the moon waits on me and as the sun I
fold

I look down at the blue planet and help it glow
Jets stream through the clouds below

I know this is just my imagination but I don't want
to let it go
I could live this life in this eternal nightâ€¦until
my eyes turn to the realitiesâ€¦and inside my
houseâ€¦I go

"The Astronaut"

Dear Larry,

I don't know what made you choose
to take your own life. But I know
I've felt that way. Underneath
the smile of the mask people
forget of the things we've loved
that went away. I feel in a way
your spirit had tiltedâ€¦pouring
all of it's happiness away. And
in the aftermath a seed of
devoured hope sprouted a flower
of shattered dreams in its place.
I know the puddle of rain you
looked in wasn't the reflection
you wished to see. And even
though it had been over a decade
since we spoke, you in so many
ways have reminded me of me. I
know you missed your dad so bad
and I've missed my mom too. They
say it's a cowardly act but they
don't know what people like us go
through. The earth turns and our
souls yearn for peace but a
restless beast is what we get to
say the least. I've tossed and
turned for some reason you've
been in multiple dreams. Friends
and alive again the way we all
hope to be. I do not look down on
you I have no idea why you did
what you did. I can only hope the

good in you shines through like
the sun through the clouds when
it comes to your kids. I think
maybe you saw a vision no one can
understand, a plan, a way to
relieve yourself of some grief
and it doesn't make you less of a
man. I hope your holding your
father's hand. In a place we all
wish to get to when we escape. I
hope there's a smile on your
face. And nothing but peace
inside of every feeling you
wanted to replace. You're not a
quitter no to me you're not. You
went to a higher placeâ€¦.you are
the astronaut.

"The Tightrope
Walker"

I couldn't look down,for the last time I did,I saw I
was surrounded by doubters.
As I trembled toe to heal trying to keep balance I
knew that if I fall there's no netâ€¦only all of my
greatest fears below waiting to devour me.
While trying to keep my eyes pointed forward and my
balance steady I thought of all the pressure I'm
enduring.
With my prior thoughts focusing on proving everyone
wrong I now only hope to survive.

The plastic fans clap their mannequin hands
I know I could make it acrossâ€¦I've done this
before.
And just then like a hidden thought I had forgotten
long ago creeping up into my brainâ€¦
I realized no matter what happens what I want is
what I should seekâ€¦accomplishâ€¦do.
And so i turn sidewaysâ€¦I put my hands in the air
and I fall.

That day I proved a point to myself and to everyone
else.
For I gave them what they want by giving myself what
I've always wanted too.
And now my name will live on and for those with open
intelligent mindsâ€¦they know.
I look upon the silicone souls with hope in my
heart.
And as I rest my head in another lifeâ€¦I'll
probably never remember the days when I used to
fear.

                              "Dear Sorrow"

Upon the winds of self hatred swept up unto me your
presence
The gloomy attic at the top of the house my soul
possesses...
A treasure chest sunk and full of moss forgotten at
the bottom of the ocean named after my lifeâ€¦my
essence

A frightening maze with ghosts I never let go of in every dark corner…more stresses

Into the abyss to wave goodbye at my most loyal friend
The bugs that infest my interior…chewing away at my structure…one day it will collapse
Shaking my head at a forever…the brick wall we all must endure…an end
A stitched up remembrance of a positive outlook…falling into all the gaps

Fingernails scraping…a desperate attempt at escaping your grasp
A camp site next to graves…where the lion cries too
A lit fire underneath a starry night…while the oak tree sways in the wind…and the nearby raven observes my gasps
Only you and I know what we go through

A slipknot tied to an innocent smile...a long lost grin
For sooner or later one of us must quit…dear sorrow
This unbeatable game we play is not about a loss or win
For if I can't feel happy today…dear sorrow…let me laugh until I love life again…maybe tomorrow?

"Even The Stars"

It's me….the man with no name
Floating on hopes and hit with bricks while trying to remain sane
By your side I stay…on a bed of nails I lay
Thoughts torturous and so morbid I in words cannot say
The tears have ran away and formed a sea of sorrow
And the hourglass continues I search in the stars for time to borrow
Behind the darkness of my eyes lives a million lies
Said to myself in a promise that is also goodbyes

Reach me touch me let me be me
For I do not know what it's like to search the fog
of my mind and see
I scream a whisper "help" from my lips
And feel you all slip away from my fingertips
An apology would be a shortcut to a place I don't
belong
I do not know who I'll be when we speak for I seek a
permanent personality before long
For years it's been this wayâ€¦almost a joke
A smile a laugh a sighâ€¦.followed by a choke
I've searched the depths of my soul for a loophole
Still continuing to sit down for cards knowing I'll
fold
I get lostâ€¦so lost in thought I break
No one knows the cold landscapes I walk in as I
count the moods on my plate
I've fallen and crawled to a place I do not know
many times
And I've walked away from a danger to find worse in
my mind
I at times cannot control my brain
I've gotten to the point I look up and even the
stars don't look the same

"Windows"

I caught myself looking into your windows todayâ€¦at
a beach of sand
A mind of waves and a heart building a castle on
land
An awakened hope with the rising of the sun
And a soul looking forward to a new day that won't
become a rerun

I found myself looking into your windows
tonightâ€¦at a nebula so bright
Holding an infinity in your handsâ€¦and in your
voice a light
Being the lifeâ€¦the beating heart of a dream
Yet no one dare take a trip deep inside because no
one remained the same at what they had seen

I saw inside your windowsâ€¦what seemed like hot red
lava
A light brighter than all of andromeda
Passion pouring into all the surrounding places and
people
Maybe I'm the only one who saw itâ€¦the somewhat
beautiful volcanic abberitional good mixed with evil

I looked outside your windowsâ€¦.to a backyard with
your children playing in it
Enjoying all they have and all there is
And as I stood up to go run with them happy and
freeâ€¦
I realized looking in and outside these windowsâ€¦I
saw a reflection of me

"The Runaways"

Julie was 17,she was a girl most would call
gorgeous,beautiful, or cute.
She was given many compliments but never
repliedâ€¦Julie was what some people would call a
"mute".
Julie didn't have a voice.
She hadn't spoke since she was 12â€¦when her
stepfather raped herâ€¦silence was her choice.
She lived a life of pain,self hatred,
disappointment,and she still smiled.
She still took life for what it wasâ€¦a beautiful
lie filled with quicksand nightmares,loneliness, and
empty miles.
She just wanted to get awayâ€¦
Far away from anything to remind her of anything of
her past days.

Bobby was 17, he wasn't very attractive but he made
up for it in his hope,love,and kind heart.
Though no one knew whyâ€¦Bobby had been born
blindâ€¦disabled from the start
He read in brail and he loved what he had read about
this beautiful world he'd never see.
About places he'd probably never be.

But he could hear…the passing of people,cars,the wind
And through all of this he still hoped…he still grinned.
He had visions though in his dreams…of running away and going to the sea.
Of being free.

One day in a story too long to be told…destiny collided in the skies.
Julie and Bobby became friends,more than friends, in love deeply even without her voice or his eyes.
They held hands and they both lived with bursting butterflies in their hearts.
She guided him and he heard her without a word a love only the two of them could ever break apart.
Julie wanted so badly to speak to him…to tell him the sights they travelled to see…but she didn't.
Bobby wanted so badly to feel her face and to feel her body….but he chose not to. So together they remained tormented…with the exception of being in love.

But although their love was untouchable and they felt immortal in ways…they had a disappearance they craved.
To runaway…to leave without a trace.
And so they packed their bags and headed for the only place that would ever matter again…the place of their end.

On the beach Bobby heard the waves and Julie finally felt free.
And so they held hands and slowly walked into the sea.
As the sun went down the sky was filled with purple orange yellow and blue.
And before they ended their lives he felt her face and said those special three words.. she finally replied "I love you too"

That was Julie and Bobby's very last day on earth…some say the story is sad.

But lifeâ€¦well life had drove them mad.â€¦for them
I'm glad.
For before they went underneath Julie did finally
speakâ€¦and Bobby well destiny had allowed him
vision for just five seconds that dayâ€¦
They lived hurt and brokenâ€¦but died strongâ€¦in
loveâ€¦and as the legendâ€¦the Runawaysâ€¦

"Come Sunset"

The horrible words that my ears were forced to hear
Instead of the kindness you can give instead
Not knowing the future and what is surely near
Just another day as we awoke and lifted our heads
out of bed

We could've laughed and had fun
But we argued and fought
Not knowing that the process had begun
Unaware of the time we still got

We could've kissed and made love
But we clenched our fist in anger
Kept each other at a distance with the shoves
Clueless of the upcoming danger

I wish we could've been betterâ€¦like we could be
But now it's too lateâ€¦we spent our last days in
liesâ€¦it was wrong
Because my fate is something we don't ponder or see
And come sunset I'll be gone

"Sweet Lover Earth"

Lift me up let's move the clouds
So the sun can shine on our skin again
Send the thunder to the distance and be proud
Soak in the rays and appreciate our friend

Put me down let's lay in the grass
And taste with me the wind she sends

Enjoy the sky…purple…pink…grey or any colors
that pass
Put your hands out and fly….pretend

Take me away and help me to find the clouds we
pushed away
Let's sail on them…the oceans of the sky
Let's close our eyes…like an air balloon is taking
us to the farthest of the day
Pretend with me…please…fly

Let's surf the stars of the night
Crashing off the nebulas like waves and don't say a
word
Now let go….float back home without a fight
But on the way blow a kiss at our sweet lover earth

                    "Make Me An Angel"

I wish I was an angel…so I could appear from the
clouds and rain
To swoop down and heal those in pain
So I could put my hands on syringes and drug addicts
will inject a cure
And in that way I help them with their demons and
they don't have to fight that battle alone anymore

I'd spread my wings and land to give shelter to the
homeless and poor
I'd change the minds of the unkind and end all the
war
I'd gather all the tears of the good people on earth
And I'd pour them on the cold hearts of those that
don't know their worth

I'd lift up the paralyzed and remind them of what it
feels like to walk
I'd heal all of those with brain damage they would
once again talk
I'd replace the memory in the elderly so they could
remember their whole lives

And I'd instill the respect in failing
marriagesâ€¦make them happy with their husbands and
wives

I would take away the sorrow of those that mourn
their once lived when gone
I'd take them to heaven so they could see who looks
on
And maybe I'm wrongâ€¦but last I'd touch my own
heart so I didn't feel so misplaced
Yes make me an angelâ€¦I would help to fix this god
forsaken place

"Beyond Paradise"

I had bowed to Gods with no faces and waited for my
response
My loyalty was but a joke to them all
They had me do all these things to awaken them as if
it was all a seance
But they gave me no answer to my calls

After all my falls my bruises my wounds I lived to
tell
Was it because of Jesus or Allah or some Hindu
deity?
I picked myself up after I fell
I was meant to get upâ€¦there was no faceless god
beside me

No God can heal your wounds like a thousand stars in
the sky
A written set of characteristics instilled in your
being
For I know on the day I dieâ€¦.
Heaven is not something I'll be seing

I remember opening up my heart and also opening up
the sky
No prayer was necessary as I felt my calling from
afar
As the stardust was rubbed onto all my scars â€¦.

I was healed and needed no symbol other than my own
sign and stars

I do not wish to downplay a belief someone holds
But I know what I've experienced in my life
To be boldâ€¦
The stars and their healing sent me beyond paradise

                         "A Porcelain Lion"

It's hard being hereâ€¦in a state of mind like mine
My heart once filled with the fire of the kings, the
beasts,and possessing the heat and life of the sun.
Now it's cold thereâ€¦I imagine the scenery being
dead trees and a chill on your spine that resides
there eternally.
My roarâ€¦once loudâ€¦once proudâ€¦now a whimperâ€¦a
cryâ€¦the sound of instability in my voiceâ€¦notice
the tear in my eye.
I don't know why.
My life is a wet dark room with leaky pipes.
The drip it will drive me insaneâ€¦the absence of
light makes me look at what's in my brain.
In my head a disappointing day.. before it even
comes to be.
Another day I didn't show upâ€¦I postponedâ€¦I
rescheduledâ€¦a day I forgot the day before.
I want to feelâ€¦I want my days back again.
I have to reignite the fire insideâ€¦wake the
comatosed beast.
I don't know how.
And as I listen to the clock tick away I remind
myself of the chariot I once drove
The plane I once piloted. The ship I once sailed.
I am not dead yetâ€¦so I cannot say I failed.
Too often though I feel I already did.
It's hard being hereâ€¦in a state of mind like mine.
I have gone from being invincibleâ€¦to a
fragileâ€¦almost porcelain lion

                         "Misery's Friend"

While dancing in the rain we had a dream
All these words to say but no lips to speak it seems
Our eyes began to bleed our vision had changed
With no sight our life was rearranged
A frozen sickle hung from our heart and chains were
on our ankles to keep us from being free
Missing both our hands we were unable to touch those
in need
Our ears rang a siren to call in the fleet
Nowhere to travel as we can't with an infinite path
of hot coals beneath our feet
Our brain in a confused state we can't think the way
we think
Our thirst unquenched by all of thisâ€¦.not a drop
of water to drink
Our guts began to ache they needed to be spilled
Our soul a hollow rockâ€¦desperately begging to be
filled
I wish you nothing but the best when I get this way
I need you by my sideâ€¦it's a good thing that you
stay
Even in my slumberâ€¦my dead flacid armsâ€¦my friend
My pen

"Lost In The Sun"

I want to smile.
With a feeling of pure joy feeding my guts.
So I can give you all the good me.
Not the broken frustrated beast I can become.
So numbâ€¦almost not an example of what I've
overcome.
I love to see you smile.
Regardless of our miles. Our disappointments.
I miss the feelings I used to feel. No longer know.
And even more I miss the freedom I saw you all have
how I observed you as you go.
It made me happy. It made me envy your charisma and
your dedication to a grin.
But deep down I remembered it allâ€¦it helped me
strive to win.

The moments I was good enough to make you laugh were
achievements .
Amongst my self hatred and griefâ€¦it was a blooming
leaf.
It meant more than my grievances.
For the changing of all my seasons changed my
needsâ€¦.but not the way I bleed
Hug me with love before I become a dust six feet
deep.
And before life is a mountain too steep
Hold close the good times we were told to keep.
My wishesâ€¦don't forget our words,our neglected
moments in time before we were forced to rewind.
I have hope that we will stand beside each other
again.
Laugh and have it carried in the wind.
Before fate pulls the trigger of its gun
Once againâ€¦usâ€¦lost in the sun

                              "Crossing Oceans"

You and I have been on this ship sailing without a
care
Standing close to the edge with our face being
soaked with the mist of a tear
Waves of all the happiness we crave crashing against
our vessel as we give each other blank stares
Our hearts beating the drum of a lost traveler, a
person with fear

The clouds forming pictures of hypocrisy and frowns
Only the fish are filled with lifeâ€¦.yet we eat
them all with a thorn handled fork and knife
Our ears penetrated violently by the winds of gloom
and a melancholy sound
Our palms filled with the beads of sweat made of
strife

I can recall a foundation we once ran on with ease
A impenetrable joy circling in our lungs
Now it's as if we are going to drown...as if we
can't breathe
And a gag of spikes is piercing our tongue

Aside each other we stood as land faded and came
Hard to believe we were brought together by fate
When all we do is stare at each other's wondering
eyes and so the bad weather came
I can't help but to think it's like crossing oceans
for us to relate

"No Forever"

I sit in this dark corner mourning the passing of
promises broke
The lies that live inside an artificial person my
love provoked
Witnesses? Only the ghosts
But I'd hate to dig the grave of the one I've cared
for the most

It eats me away like a slow torture in my brain
cells
My memory? A strong encouragement that didn't end
well
Somehow somewhere there's the person that I fell in
love with
A human with a cage outside her heart and too many
emotions to play withâ€¦I think I'm sick

It's very possible I will end it but I doubt it with
all the defaults I came with
I've gone insane and lost the mood that told me the
bad times would fade quick
She doesn't care.. like loving air
I breathe her in and my hope fades yet stays there

I think of the softness I knowâ€¦truth is it's
hardened like a garden of concrete it stays still
Am I her prey? Just the next kill?
Yet I exhale a memory that won't disappear and speak
in a deaf ear
My heart it feels the fear

The lie that no one can deny

Only to express in a sign
For those lost or clever
The most painful truthâ€¦.there is no forever

"Sad Horse"

Amy was only 7 when she begged
her father to get her a pony. He
hestiated he waitedâ€¦he gave
her the pony on her birthday.
She was excited to say the
least. She loved the pony
immediately. She named him
Shadow. Her and shadow played
together most of her young days.
I guess you could say they had a
bond.

Together they enjoyed many sunsets, many full moons,
many stormy days as well. Shadow watched Amy grow
into a teenager. And unfortunately as she became a
teenager he had to spend less time with her as she
was with her friends alot. Shadow didn't like her
friends. Not because he had to share his girl with
them but because she seemed very distant and
different. Not just to him but to her family as
well.

Soon he barely saw her at all. And one dayâ€¦not
ever again. Her friends had introduced her to a drug
with a special name. She had been missing for weeks.
Her parents were worried sick and so was Shadow. On
one sad morning she was found in the woods with a
needle in her arm and a wax bag in her palm.She was
gone.

Shortly after this horrible situation Shadow became
sick. He lost his energy and his happiness and when
her parents took him to an animal doctor they were
told he had cancer. He enjoyed a few more weeks if

lonely sunsets on his own. Missing her. And finally
one day he went to sleep and never woke.

Many people say that love is pain. That love is only
skin deep. But for Shadow his love for Amy was much
more. This was proof that love is fate. Because both
Amy and her horse died of the same thing. Shadow
died and became sick because of his broken heart.
Amy died of an overdose falling in love with a
substance. But the wax bag found in her cold palm
was stampedâ€¦with the wordsâ€¦.'sad horse'â€¦more
than irony I'm sure.

"The Road To Happiness"

I started my car with it full of all those that said
they loved me   .
The day was young and we smiled at the sun
It was time to get rid of all these negative
feelings
The roads we travelâ€¦some paved some dirt and
gravel
We drove through all the states seeing all the
beauty and wonderful sights
We were so happyâ€¦there were no bad moments,no
arguments,no fights.
The days we spent on that trip were so exciting and
created a lightness in our hearts.
We pulled over on the darkest of nights to marvel at
the stars
There were no liesâ€¦no disputesâ€¦nothing but us
feeling alive as we shed our skin with a grin
And finally in California we sat in our car on top
of a big cliff watching the sun come up.
And so with the front wheel barely on land I put the
car in drive and hit the gas.
During our long descent I saw all of them
disappearâ€¦they were never there to begin with.
But I swear even though I died alone as I fell
towards the groundâ€¦.i felt lovedâ€¦I felt

alive...the last thing I did was smile….the road
to happiness

"Garden Of Ghosts"

Sometimes I wish I could sleep forever…not in
death
But to breathe in the people in my dreams' breath
To become free

I've planted the seeds….in everyone…and gave
them a choice
Feed the flowers inside…or let them grow and
wither…to fade without a voice
To become powerless

When I wonder….do they hear the echoes of my
footsteps on the freshly cut grass
Do they see my tears on their tombstone…a whisper
of death in my laugh
To become saddened

A heart of glass….i fear to show
So broken…tearing my soul apart with it's shards
of all I've known
To become scared

Losing purpose…a skeleton in clothes
For if I go…I'll grow…a white rose
To join the garden of ghosts

"The Fading Of Shadows"

I sat here before…you sat next to me
A blissful moment that has gone by
A moment never duplicated for anyone else to see

Do I hold the bad up to the light? Or put the good
into the dark shadow behind my heart so it dies when
I die?

I walked there beforeâ€¦ you walked along my side
A few minutes we existed together
A portion of time in life written inside my heart's
diary for me to hide
Tucked away inside the darkest part of my soul until
the end of forever

I had rested my head there beforeâ€¦you lie next to
me
At least an hour no one could ever take away
One twenty fourth of a date on the calender we were
close to free
Do I forget this hour? Or stick it in my darkest
desolate area in my brain to be thought about on
another day?

I flew this dayâ€¦you didn't come with me
A tragedy to others as I pass the crow the dove the
clouds stars and sparrows
Others cryâ€¦with no reason.â€¦I am filled with glee
I took you all with meâ€¦hidden in the darkest part
of meâ€¦and there is no fading of shadows

"Kismet"

Life is not a long journey
Rather a short adventure
All the characters will give you sight
All you can do is make yourself blind
The souls sent to light up your soul come and
goâ€¦and so will you
Hold that lightâ€¦pass on that light until you
become dark again
All those that receive your light reflect it
Onto the world like a prism of what the world never
saw you as
The hate and degrading stops not by prayers to a god
But in proof you meant well

In the search for happiness….the blind did not look.
Those reflecting light are full of happiness with that as their purpose.
I only sadden for those that have given away all their light and remained dark…like me
To leave behind kind deeds and a shadow of their silhouettes in the hearts of those with heads hung low.
I hide in the darkest corner of sorrow…many days I sleep there.
Knowing I've held souls in my palms full of light…but I did not see.
I only feel….i watch the stars shine…feel the earth move…and hope the sun rises again….sometimes.
Lately I feel the stars worry for me.
Unsettled staring back at me.…waiting for me to reflect my light for the lives that depend on me the way I depend on the sun.
But my blindness…my light has been extinguished
I only hope someone with light finds my corner I hide in.
Before the earth turns one last time. And the stars reflect their worry once again on my darkness
And kismet takes me to my next short adventure…

"I'm Sorry"

To be remembered, you write something that makes people feel like they're not so alone, like they're not so cold, like you hurt like they do, and then you die.

To be loved, you speak kind words even when bound in chains in your mind, so they don't feel so restrained, so they can dance upon your hidden sadness, and then you die.

To be respected, you smile upon the field of snakes, you step lightly through their slithering, you whistle to them as they coil around your heart, and then you die.

To be honored,you bow to invisible gods,like they
control it all,like they care about your soul enough
to show you mercy,and then you die.

To be free,you release yourself from this cage,you
break down the gates, like you have somewhere to
run,like you know how you'll be the shining star,to
join the lions in the sky,and you leave this
knowledge behind and title it "I'm sorry"

"Into Exile"

I remember the day well when I sent my heart into
the wind
Blowing away like a summer wish from a little boy
with a full grin
Tears creating a lake at my feet for the memories to
swim in
The clouds all shaped like a new beginning

The table I sat at lonesome and conversing with my
soul with relativity
The echoes throughout the room remind me of the sea
Waves of beauty seen the same way once but never
againâ€¦in a short lifetimeâ€¦me
The walls holding about an empty shellâ€¦hear me
flee

The floor I fell toâ€¦acceptingâ€¦a comfortable
pillow
With sudden flashbacks of my bleeding knees held in
each creaseâ€¦pain skipping through its meadows
A pain that hears my screams for helpâ€¦the glue of
depression holding me down as I billow
To a fresh dramatic new shadow

Yes I remember the day I fellâ€¦.into a new faceâ€¦a
new nameâ€¦a new smile
A human structure similar to a shellâ€¦hear me from
miles

Picked from the sand made of a broken man,a thought
I had since I was a juvenile
A piece of beauty gone from this life…into a
temporary exile

                              "The Glass Castle"

I sip you down one more time…to numb the pain
inside
To help me forget about my minds dimensions
To help me to not look in the mirror…and see my
reflection
To help me get a grip on myself when I feel all this
hatred towards love and life and it seems so
pretentious

I take more and more chugs…to calm my soul
To help me find the darkness of my dreams
To help put me to sleep…the light hurts my third
eye it seems
To help blind me to this world…so I could survive
another day…to help this conflicted mind lean

I drink my life away….because I've lost purpose
To help ease the pressure of being a leader or an
inspiration
To help walk away from this torment I'm facing
To help bring this to an end…this running in
place…it's my own self I've been racing

I take the last sip from my cup…I see my
reflection
A sad story I won't turn around… an invisible
crown creating no hassle
They could call me a quitter,a loser,an asshole
But the king dies more with each view of my
reflection…in my glass castle

                              "Tortured Smiles"

I think deep down…you're like me…somewhere
inside you've died
Wearing your mask of smiles to cover the tears you
cry
Your true face forever denied
In this dreary world you hide

The quietest days are to me so very loud
So many voices and doing what my mind allows
A bit of sunshine peeks through our cloud
We try to soak it in…but in the end we're not
proud

Our clock ticks and we pace wait for another change
Write out books and leave dirty fingertips on each
page
One filled with sadness one happiness one rage
Bowing out gracefully and stepping off our stage

Mental feet are blistered from walking all these
miles
Morphine numb metaphorically…but the pain will
return in awhile
The grandfather clock ticks growing impatient for me
and my sanity to reconcile
Yeah you are just like me…living terrified to
laugh…hoping they don't see our tortured smiles

                                        "Dear
                                        Butterfly"

In this big grassy field I sit….watching you fly
free.
With your wings creating panoramic views against the
sun.
I myself cannot move far… in a way I miss how you
were in the jar.
In life we cannot predict the outcomes nor the
questions and answers.

Your friendship…i miss it so after i let you
go…it eats away my brain like a cancer.
But deep down…I know you were meant to go…to
give the world your glow
Your colors reside in my mind...I can only think of
the good times
Because the bad times were very bad…I was forced
to watch from this field I've been placed
in...hoping those without hearts wouldn't leave you
crushed to dust
In my mind…I've become your protector
But I cannot be yours…our bond has changed...like
a flip from a projector
Although I still wish to have you sit next to me as
the skies change…I don't want it to be the same
Such a shame…for I am tired of the blame
I am comfortable wondering what pretty flower you'll
find to sit on…under what color sky
Than to try to force a lie…it is not I
So one last time I'll sit here…here watching your
silhouette in the full moon
In the middle of this field…a lion in a
cage…hoping it gets unlocked sometime soon
Dear butterfly…goodbye

"The Crow And
The Dove"
 Co-written
 by Blair
 Kranch

As I flew from his trembling hands I could not look
back. My delicate white wings stretched out and as
the wind whistled through the flowers below me I
felt freed. I saw the world, bright and vast. The
skies above me were vibrant blues while the ground
below me looked soft and gentle.
I flew free for quite some time. It was as if every
ounce of my feathers tingled with adventure, but
eventually I grew tired & was ready to discover a

place to rest my wild wings. In the distance I saw a glorious tree; one I wanted to be my place of calming. It was wild and it grew freely, with branches that were like outstretched arms, calling me home.

I nestled comfortably into the branches & there he was as if he had been waiting lifetimes to find comfort in his brand new heaven, in a world he had been so eager to explore, just as I, too, had been desperately seeking to find comfort, in the unknown.

I sat here waitingâ€¦.looking down from this large oak tree. I was patient for something but I didn't know what. And my wing was no longer broken. I could fly away. But i chose to stay. I often held my head down and had visions while in deep thought. Dreams to me, just an imagination running wild of a love I'll never feel. A loneliness broken and a mind occupied by love. I missed some of those that flew away while I was broken. Maybe I'll see them one day. Or maybe I'll rest in this version of heaven I've lived in. On my own and unloved. Just above and watching days and nights fade.

And as I rested my wings after soaring for awhile, I saw her. She landed on a branch across from mine. She was beautiful. Even more beautiful than everything I've viewed from above. I made my way to her side.

"Hello, I'm a crow" I said with a low hesitant voice.
"Hello, crow. I am a dove. What brings you here?" I asked, curious to hear what he had to say.
"I had been broken. I finally flew again...but I've been here by myself since then. What has brought you here?" I wondered.
"I was set free after being trapped for so long, but I grew tired and needed to find a place of peace." I looked at her so fondly. And I said "Well it's very peaceful here. Maybe you could stay here with me? We could fly together and i can show you some of the nearby places to rest and enjoy the scenery"

"I'd love to stay with you." I answered him calmly but inside I was bursting. I knew, from that very moment, I wanted to stay with him forever.

And that is exactly what happened. The crow and the dove spent the rest of their days exploring each other and life and all that the tree in the sky had to offer. They were no longer held down or broken. They were fate at it's finest.

1. "Alive"

I open up the shadesâ€¦.hello sun
 On the table in front of meâ€¦gunpowder inside an
 eternal dream
Tears made of disposed goals hide my sight from my
friendâ€¦my gun
Text messages vibrate my electronic life saverâ€¦but
none of it is what it seems

The liesâ€¦.forever wrapped up nicely with smiles of
deceit
I have grownâ€¦so much I know it's ok to pity me
These moodsâ€¦they seem like a million of meâ€¦they
take me off my feet
In truthâ€¦I feel like I digest them in waysâ€¦I
feed

They say I'm beautifulâ€¦a beautiful heartâ€¦a
monster in my mind
I can't but feel like a western sunset
I once shined for a dayâ€¦but then it left in the
mirrorâ€¦and I began committing self inflicted
murderous crimes
Another day no one can see in meâ€¦another one I'd
like to forget

I feel shaking in my shoulders and feetâ€¦the gun a
boulder on my tongue
Weighing down my only way to survive
And as my finger presses down on the trigger of my
gunâ€¦

My mood changes...I made it once againâ€¦and in an
odd wayâ€¦I now feel more alive

2. "1,237 Stars"

Here I am where it all started.
Me on my backâ€¦so brokenâ€¦so confusedâ€¦searching
for something I don't think I'll ever find.
A lost gaze gave me minutes of peaceâ€¦for once.
I began to think of you.
A whirlpool of feelings touched my soul like soft
fingertips.
Caressing my distress into a purring submission.
A multi colored aura floated just above my skin.
I loved my life this moment in time.
My eyes never moved as much as the floating my body
felt.
My heart became flourescent and lit up my spirit
like a carnival thrived inside of me.
I cleared my throat and breathed in air with you
still on my mind.
The oxygen felt like a feather journeying its way
into my lungs as they felt like balloons levitating
to the clouds.
My brain massaged by remembering your voiceâ€¦your
voice imprinted into the cement and scars I bare.
My hollow bones were drifting me up into the cosmos
like my love for you was a rocketship.
Youâ€¦you've become the stars.
Glowing in the dark and so beautiful to look at.
Your presence is my favorite constellation.
You've become my universeâ€¦I want to explore
youâ€¦to see your mystery and feel my lack of
gravity.
I raise my head off the grassâ€¦I'm sure I'm in
love.
In love with youâ€¦as sure as there's one thousand
two hundred thirty seven stars in the sky
tonightâ€¦time for bed.

I wonder what happens to love lost…
Does that energy soar to the nearest dying star?
Will it shoot into the life of someone in need?
Or does it soak into the veins of a tree…does it
bleed?

I think about what happens the all the disposed
hate?
Will it drip into the nearest running spring?
Will it flood the home of someone filled with greed?
Or will it be drunk in by a tender soul and plant a
seed?

I ponder on what becomes of departed hope….
Does it spread its wings like a million fireflies to
the nearest flower petal?
Will it ignite the spirit of a lonely teenager lost
in thought?
Or will it launch a bomb and hit our world with all
it's got?

I want to know what will happen when we forget
faith…
Does it turn it's back to its new enemy?
Will it cause us to fall into blades of grass made
of thorns?
Or will it awaken a light to drift us into a place
unwarned?

Because of my questions under all of life's
circumstances…
I try not to lose any of it at all.
It was all here for a reason whether we were filled
with smiles or living with hearts torn.
There is no forgotten departure.

4. "Sadness At The
    Window Sill"

Come on and feel my soul
Gain wisdom from my pain
For those you loveâ€¦.hold them close
Before life scratches out their name

I sit here on the window sill looking out at all
this life
Waiting for carissa to pull in to say hi
Maybe that's why I fail to feel alive
I'm waiting on the deadâ€¦like a confused
animalâ€¦who never had a chance to say goodbye

Days go byâ€¦I'm back at the window sill as the
skies pour rain
I recall dancing with my mom in storms like this
So this is my moment of joyâ€¦a wonderful
memoryâ€¦left in my brain
I imagine she will invite me back outsideâ€¦but she
no longer lives

Weeks laterâ€¦.I sit here againâ€¦ watching birds
fly together
Their life is like mine
One dayâ€¦one of them will dieâ€¦ending their
forever
But survivingâ€¦being freeâ€¦is all that's in their
mind

Come on and feel my soul
Gain wisdom from my pain
If you love meâ€¦hold me close
Before I'm gone like I had never came

5. "Ashes In The
    Wind"

I know I am nothing but a man
With dreams and empty hands
Looking for someone to care
Staring at the air
Searching for peace in my soul
Getting sucked into a dark hole
Trying to maintain a balanced mind
With moods destroying half of my time

This crime I commit without a conscience
This betrayal of all I love
The turning of my back to the world
And the spitting in the face of life
But I sit in this dark room with my heart beating
slowly
Talking to myself in debate
No don'tâ€¦no don'tâ€¦no don't
You won'tâ€¦you won'tâ€¦you won't

I don't want to dieâ€¦
Still these thoughts degrade meâ€¦betray me
There's no reason to stayâ€¦
But there's plenty of reasons to stayâ€¦at least
today
But tomorrow what will I sayâ€¦how will I feel
Staring at the ceiling with the tears of hidden
worlds
Worlds no one lives in but me
I hope I dieâ€¦.

Please don't turn away from me
My mind is killing me
I can make itâ€¦I will make it
I'll keep myself here for the torture
To breathe smiles into those in need
With a sad frown awaiting their departure
But promise pleaseâ€¦if I ever give in
Don't hate meâ€¦understandâ€¦and throw my ashes in
the wind

6. "The House Of
    Ghosts"

I elevated towards the ceiling…through the ceiling
Without any feeling
I saw him lay below me looking up at me intently
Yet I felt nothing mentally
Strange…I always felt everything
Every burst of wind every shine of the sun every
human being
I felt a sudden pain in my body in my heart
And then I realized I had become a star….

I fell into this deep dark hole without warning
And it hurt me so bad…a pain that came with
learning
I saw him above not moving at all
I felt it all so hard I looked up and began to crawl
Oddly…I never felt anything
Not heartbreak not abuse not even a bee sting
And suddenly i began to burn…to stink and swell
And i realized i was in hell….

I stood up and brushed myself off...standing in the
living room
I was hoping dinner was done soon
I saw him beside me…looked just like me
Nothing much to see
I looked for a moving person anywhere in sight
But there was no one this night
The door was open…I tried to push it closed
And then I realized I was a ghost….

I lie there dead…..i took it all away
To rot and decay
I saw nothing but black
And yet I did feel empty i wouldn't take it back
I think all of me has left
To share what I've held inside….a gift
I was in life nothing but a host
In my very own…house of ghosts

7. "Where Did You
   Go?"

There was a cloud we searched for together…raining
on another world somewhere in a small town
A place filled with full syringes and empty
dreams...but take a picture of your prom dress and
wedding gowns
The puddles walked on by generations….reflections
of sorrow to be seen... a sorry excuse to drown
I look to the corner…car engines in ear...a dry
mouth…not any hope to be found

We had found a sun to beat on us…shining down with
might
My imagination...an innocent boy and girl fly a kite
Tell your friends of the fight
The battle of those who forgot they had a choice…a
right

I clinched my eyes to see the snow pile up high
So brisk in our souls…the disposable sighs
I walk to the sidewalk and see a man and a
child…waiting for spring nights
"Hello" the man says…not knowing my disgust held
deep…for I am not right

I walk into the doors….cries are heard in small
weeps of what was before
Another day of this…another soul "flies high" but
sinks the hearts of those that adore
I can't cry anymore
Another heroin addict that hit the floor

Wings are spread all over our dark clouds…people
not knowing the pain they left below
The children left in the darkness after they see the
glow
This an old and boring show…
Don't you see? All we can think anymore is where did
you go?

8. " Open Field
    Daydream"

Today…I closed my eyes…I let my brain drift away in the middle of a sunflower filled field.
The sun's rays healed every scar on my body and gave my soul energy.
It sank into my skin like a magical lotion sent from the sky.
I felt so handsome... so flawless…I felt alive…I felt like I mattered.
The grass and flowers grew…wrapping around my body like I belonged with them…like I was just as beautiful.
My brain saw so vividly into truth…I became stabilized…i felt happy…so happy a tear would forcefully flee from my eye.
A nearby river formed into a wave crashing against me but all the life held me up.
All the animals nearby flocked into a mass around me.
I held my arms out receiving the hug from the sun.
A crow and dove landing on each of my wrists as wolves and lions rest at my feet.
It felt good…too good…I opened my eyes.

Tonight…i opened my eyes…i let my heart drift away in the middle of a sunflower filled field.
The moon elevated me into the arms of angels.
They told me they loved me…I believed them.
They plucked stars from the night canvas and fed them to me.
I ate them until the universe sat inside me.
The honesty of the cosmos leaked from my throat.
And off my tongue came the words of a believer…of a fighter…of a lover.
I spoke hope into the hopeless…breathed breath of the winds of Saturn into the hot scorching souls.
I sneezed black holes to absorb all sadness.
And wiped my nose on a napkin turning it into a clear blue crystal holding all of time.
I need to rewind….I closed my eyes

I woke to my very life. To myself and my girlfriend and our children standing in a nearby parking lot.
And I realized for the first time…even in my

wildest dreams…life was better right where I was…enjoy life.

9. "The Great Disappointment"

This long windy road of doubt has brought me here
For I have took the train to sorrow and sailed on a giant tear
I have looked in wonder at the sky
Talking to the stars as clouds dropped a raindrop in my eye
I have laughed at frustration and disowned all rage
I read things I wrote and held tight my life on a page
Photographs have kept my mind adrift to dream
The ghosts of days gone by…the memories closer than they seem
Blistered feet and calluses cover my hands…all in my brain
Billions of ticks twirled slowly down the drain
Happiness residing in the ink…but only after spilling regret
A mess of a human…I guess about more than I forget
I took a sledgehammer to the walls of others…gained trust
I stepped through an open book too hard to read…they give up
My eyes have seen many hiding places…travelling by in cars
A place I'll sit…close by…to feel far
I've flown planes over landscapes in souls forgotten
Cloudy and hard to land…lanterns thrown out to eat…gone rotten
The window sill held my breath in the sand
I drew I love you with my hand…for a stranger but not the reflection of that man
I wish I could stop opening up my chest…for others to feed
My heart has lost weight…i still let it bleed
But on this road what will i leave behind? For them to find

To show the world needs the kind…it's a short
amount of time
In eternity…a segment
I look up at the road…still long…in
life…sometimes that's the great disappointment

10. " I Am The
Storm"

I have stolen a thousand lives
And my existence is wished upon but rarely seen
I am the result of a wonderful dream
I let off steam
You see me where the sun shines and the ocean turns
light blue
You have seen me in you
I am the main focus of a picture
I will make your friends happy and your enemies mad
I am the opposite of sad
People strive to have me…to possess me
Every single day I am what someone wants to see
In fact I am what someone wants to be
I am a portrait of happiness and a display of
caring,love,and trust
When you want to reign on your despair…I am the
rain that comes with the storm
In reality I am the storm…I am a smile

11. " The Man On The
Corner"

A little while ago… I walked down the
street…step by step…watching where I walk.
While in blank thoughts a voice came from the corner
of a street I knew well.
"Hey bro" a man said to me.

I looked up to see an unshaved man with dirty
clothes smiling at me.
He looked familiar…but I couldn't recall who he
was.
I nodded my head at him to not be rude.
I think the fact that I didn't stop upset him.
His expression on his face changed and he looked sad
or maybe even surprised I didn't converse with him.

The thought of this moment haunted my mind all my
days and nights.
Who was this man and what did he want from me?
Did we know each other? Should I have stopped to
talk to him?
I always seem to be in a rush and I feel like I
sometimes neglect people I know.
But he looked homeless or on some sort of
drug….yet there was something in his face…his
eyes…that I knew.

Just a few days later….I received a call from one
of my childhood friends.
They told me how one of my old close friends had
hung himself and asked if I was going to the
viewing.
I said I would.
What a sad moment. Me and him were so close for so
many years.
He tried to reach out to me through social media
asking for my number.
I ignored him…as if the changes I made in my life
made me better than those I once evolved with.
I didn't give him a second of my time.

Just two days later… I went to the viewing. As I
walked through the doors I noticed it was only me
and my friend who called me to come.
When I grew the guts to walk up to the casket I did.
In a sudden awakening I looked at him…I realized
He was the man on the corner. He was my old best
friend.
He was the face I barely recognized on the streets.

Until this day…I cry from time to time.

I could have stopped to talk to that man I thought
was a stranger.
Though time moves fast and faces change…people are
worth your time.
Maybe if I'd have just responded different his life
and death would have been different.
I'll never forget those I grew with…I'll never
forget the man on the corner.

12. "The Boy Under The
     Table"

Scream your obscenities at her…belittle her
As if he is not there…as if he doesn't matter
That's his hero you put your hands on
The boy under the table will save her world

Be absent from his life….abandon him daily
As if he wasn't waiting for you…but your promises
don't matter
That's his heart you abuse
The boy under the table will one day change the
world

He doesn't know the world…only what he's been
shown
As if his mind is his home… as if he's alone
That's his mentality that is warped and changed
The boy under the table will want to end his world

Under the table he is a superhero…in his head
Under the table he is lonely…in truth
Under the table everyone has forgot his face…again
Fathers…the boy under the table was me… make
yours your world

13. "Lost While
     Looking"

Sometimes we run out of words to say
A look or a silence on display
Neon lights flicker outâ€¦the ones that shined
bright on better days
We just look at the sky and watch dawn and dusk fade
away
Some cross their fingers some pray
Just to feel their light even though they know it
won't stay
Optimistic revelations exist in the presence of a
stray
Pessimistic revolutions arise in those that will
surely decay
We swirl in a whirlpool of attention sure to betray
Just to sink just to disappear to be cliche
Reflections become portraits of regret and dismay
Never holding the knowledge of how you're
viewedâ€¦most by a yesterday
Sometimes we forget what we will hold tight today
A passion extinguishedâ€¦like setting fire to a
bouquet
Our brain sizzles in the sunâ€¦like eggs on a pan
Tomorrow's foodâ€¦whether woman or man
In your palm do you hold your life span?
Or the ghost of anotherâ€¦a brother or a mother or a
lover?
Either way one day life will hold the pillow leaving
you smothered
To join those that had faces disappear into the
cloudsâ€¦the forgotten cup at the back of the
cupboard
When I goâ€¦I'd love to knowâ€¦when i was searching
for myself was i collared
When i would talk was i heard
Was i lost while looking at a reflection no one has
remembered?

                            14. " Starlit
                                 Soul"

How did you know my soul was listening

When you stepped out of my dreams
I saw your eyes glistening
Lighting up my heart more than it seems

I've been confused with your kindness
Lifeâ€¦has left me questioning all I know
As I've been scarred by the mindless
And still somehow was blessed with your glow

I look to the skies and thank every shining star for
letting me experience your soul
For leaving their best with me
So you can make me feel whole
And I believe the gleam of your smile has helped me
to once again see

I feel your skinâ€¦a soft shell
The tide rises in my heart
I fall into your moonlight and you help me to propel
And my dream lies next to meâ€¦my light in the dark

I've heard your voice in the echoes of the past
I followed the sounds of every constellation you
possess
I was guided to you and I laughed
All that painâ€¦now I know what all that pain meant

We've been through the wormholes and dropped from
the sky onto each others doorsteps
So the pain can leaveâ€¦we now have control
And if it takes all I have left
I'll hold forever your ever so healing starlit soul

15. "My Worthless
     Heart"

Just me and youâ€¦the sun shiningâ€¦the sky blue
A monster lurking â€¦. A creature that wants to
destroy me
I look for reasssurance around every corner
For I don't want to lie cold at the coroner

I am sensitiveâ€¦ I am brokenâ€¦I smile for show
I have hiddenâ€¦deep insideâ€¦a forest that no one
knows
It protects me from the monstersâ€¦so it's there
that I go
So I could cryâ€¦so I could love myselfâ€¦in the
shadows

I apologizeâ€¦for being the burden I am to you
Sometimes I look through the cracks in my
wallsâ€¦but the monster is peeking through
My fingertips searchâ€¦a hand to holdâ€¦my life to
save
I'm so sorryâ€¦I just want to be lovedâ€¦I want to
be safe

I am weakâ€¦but I am strongâ€¦I still have courage
to share this all with you in trust
My monsterâ€¦.full of rust
My dark soul waits on stars to decideâ€¦.will I hide
If my worthlessâ€¦insecureâ€¦monster heart will be
crushedâ€¦and I have to admit I'm nothing without
you

16. "I Have No Name"

I have no name
For one day I'll be just a face in your history
A boy who grew to be a man who grew to be a mystery
I wore sunglasses with my umbrella open on a sunny
day
And they laughed and were angered by my tearsâ€¦by
my mind's ways
I shed sorrow until it seemed like a storm of
rainâ€¦inside I had given up
And I waited for headlights through the
teardropsâ€¦someone to pick me up
I smiled for their happiness I wanted for their
peace
Deep in the dark abyss of my life reside the same
tormenting beast
Crumbling in the darkness of an unsaid word I fell

No crutch no embrace to wish me well
I had a dream that I was handsome and appreciated
and all my loved ones thought I was the best
Then I awoke to the uncomforting reality to deal
with that pest
Why couldn't I have stayed in that dream?
Where things were betterâ€¦where i was
betterâ€¦where things aren't as they seem
Maybe in some parallel universe my mirrors aren't
shattered to pieces of disgust
My robotic life isn't filled with decay and distrust
I can awaken to a new day forgetting all I know
Until thenâ€¦I'm meâ€¦I'm hurtâ€¦I'm the same
Yes one day I will disappear into thin airâ€¦I have
no name

17. "One Day Left"

The old man awoken in his hospital bed with a
feeling of clarity. He was on his death bed and
could feel deep down in the ever so tired soul of
his that today would be his last day. He saw from
the open window the glowing sun and felt that it
comforted him. That it could listen to all he had
left to say.

"I have grown tired. Tired of fighting for an
invisible purpose. I had so many moments of strength
I forgot that it is inevitable that I end up here.
Forgive me for my lack of caring. But I know
nowâ€¦it's ok to be weak sometimes. I've found some
very caring souls. I duplicated them. So I could be
better. I've sailed on the rays of the sun to an
island of tranquility to ease my troubled mind. My
heartâ€¦oh my heart is yours. But sadly my mind is
eager for release. Please tell my children to love
in a world of hate. To love themselves any way they
can. And youâ€¦please continue to shine down on all
those with weeping souls, those lost along the road,
and those who are trapped in their mind. Never feel
left behindâ€¦they'll always come back for you if

they love you. Even those gone like I will soon be.
And remember that I love youâ€¦ ever since we met. I
have piloted a plain into an open field of
flowersâ€¦i named that field after you. I loved
youâ€¦like the wind loves a birds wings. I will hold
you close wherever I go. And I'll see you in a
different lifeâ€¦or in heavenâ€¦or in my last
secondâ€¦.whatever theory is trueâ€¦I'll love you
there."

He closed his eyes seconds later for the last time.
He died peacefully. That old man will be me. That
sunâ€¦.is you.

18. "Desolate"

Kill me insideâ€¦until nothing remains
A horror pumps through my veins
Another end to something beautiful
We sipped the hope so fastâ€¦the cup no longer full
Now I sit here in a barren wasteland
With white roses in one and a noose in the other
hand
But I have no planâ€¦just shortening time to figure
out my life
The sky holding above me a knife
I pace the corridors punching my fist through walls
My splintered skin a sign of the outcome of this all
I've lost the thought of a win
I twist around in loops with or without youâ€¦when
does a standing still of a smile begin?
I try so hard to be what you want me to be
But with teary eyes and a dark cloud above me it's
hard to see
I feel so muchâ€¦I want to be loved like everyone
else
My efforts are a wave to a blind manâ€¦a penny to
the wealth
So I remain jogging uphillâ€¦wanting a stroll
amongst the trees
My mindâ€¦my heart has brought me to my knees

In moments like this please pick me up and don't give up on me

In a happy worldâ€¦. A world where you are happy is where my smile wishes to be

I float in a wave of my own

You are the waterâ€¦your happiness is my home

But when will I be good enough for that to make you grin?

So I could feel freeâ€¦so I could do more than floatâ€¦I want to swim

It's up to youâ€¦in your powerâ€¦to find my cure by making me worth somethingâ€¦.without me making a mess of it

Please save meâ€¦usâ€¦I feel destroyed in between spinsâ€¦I feel desolate

19. "Colorful World"

I woke up to realize I was in a world I never knew

A world where I don't know if love is a phaseâ€¦or just a phrase.. but it never seems to be true

Where respect is like the lionsâ€¦endangeredâ€¦nearly extinct

And loyalty is like a diamondâ€¦sometimes not as pure as you think

Faithfulness is a sometimes hobbyâ€¦only displayed for social media merits

A world where trust is almost heart suicideâ€¦leaving it as valuable as torn fabrics

Honorâ€¦a rarityâ€¦an unspoken word amongst all the absurd

Hateâ€¦complaintsâ€¦the only words still heard

I can't feel in this worldâ€¦it's forbidden

I leave no stone unturnedâ€¦I need to know what is hidden

The fall of a society in my eyes and I don't think I can make a change

I just write and hope someone who agrees reads this page

I look to the stars and askâ€¦

Please bring back the old, vibrant, colorful world I
used to know…

20. "Orion's Tears"

On a purple skied evening…
I sit at the table sipping tea mixed with my
favorite stardust
Who shines for me?

Running through my blood stream… the pain of a
million broken hearted angels
In my brain…the thoughts of tortured demons
Who understands the existence of me?

My heart transformed into the imaginative heavens
Floating in a cosmic eternity
When will my end be?

My soul waving at innocent smiles
My room empty
When will the loneliness end?

On my neck the hands of Polaris
Under my feet the heat of Sirius
When will I illuminate the world?

My hope faded like ancient graveyard burial stones
My eyes…wide and open to see
When will I awaken?

The raindrops hit the rooftop
A smile shines on my face…brighter than the sun
Orion's tears

21. "The Burning
     Man"

As I lie next to you in silence…I wonder do you
want to be somewhere else with someone other than
me?
In the morning when you wake…isn't being in my
arms good enough? Am I not the face you wish to see?
Inside it turns my stomach crashing against my
butterflies and drowning them in the waves of a
reckless sea.
And in my heart I want you to love me…but if you
don't shall I hold you for as long as I could? Or
should I set you free?

In this moment of quiet disruption I see a blank
stare on your face.
I feel joy in your presence… although you seem to
be in a different place.
I am selfish I believe…grasping for one more
special moment to hide like treasure…almost like a
chase.
But as days go by I think…did your love for me
die? Is this not a chase but a race that will leave
me displaced

I reach over for your hand and grab it
tightly…please hold my hand in return.
For every time I doubt you feel the same I can feel
my heart burn.
It hurts it breaks it wants so badly to learn.
What do I have to do to make you love me back…so I
can receive this heart of yours I yearn?

As more days go by and inside I cry…nothing puts
out the flames.
There's nothing worse than needing the love of
someone who doesn't feel the same.
It shakes my soul to submission…it sends pain
throughout my brain.
Each time I die again…every time with "the burning
man" as my name

22. "The
     Cocoon"

In here I sit alone… in a world of empty
answers…with just a matter of time before I go
home.
I've cried for pretenders who will believe their
lies until I'm gone.
I know it won't be long. …
Until my wings open…I do not feel wrong for
leaving…for flying towards the sun.

Since my birth I've known… the smiles on their
faces are forced…with hearts made of stone.
Their stories are of false living…their lies only
existing because they are condoned.
I know it won't be long. …
Until my colorful wings are spread to fly into the
barrel of a gun.

Since I've aged I could see…the mental language
perceived as free.
The loneliness in we.
I know so very soon…
I will hold my wings out straight and get crushed in
this room.

Since I've died I could feel…their cries added
blue to my wings.
I myself have become them…believed their
beliefs…such pretentious things.
There is no soon…
I was dying and alone…right from the cocoon.

23. "One Day"

I want to be free of me
My insecurities…my sadness
Can they leave and give me just enough time to see?
With clarity…with truth…without madness

I want to know what thoughts I think are acceptable
and real

My blurry vision…my past
I feel so much…at once…I'm not even sure which
is the right way to feel
I wish…my brain…could be put into some sort of
cast…to fix me….to repair the cracks

I have let off my fingertips my dreams
The white rose…that grew from concrete
But I don't want to be beautiful…I want to wither
back into the seams
So I could have peace…and I don't have to worry of
being stepped on…underneath someone's uncaring
selfish feet

I wish the stars would answer my wishes
The peace…the relief that I can be confident when
I enough to stay…
I hope after all the tears,the laughter,the hoping,
the kisses…
That I could be ok with myself one day.

24.   "Vertigo Love"

I saw the fire in my heart reflect off your blue
eyes
The enchantment of the wild ran it's course
The gift of the stars and the deepest of space
Anti-gravity broken by the fall
On my way down I had the most beautiful of sights
Your body was my amusement park…my favorite ride
Your face an undiscovered rain forest filled with
flowers never seen…a place I wanted to take a
picture of
The wind…it blew me into a million different
directions
But i never lost comfort…i just went along with it
My stomach felt as though a friendly soul was
tickling it and it made my soul giggle too
With you…the world had brightened even on the
darkest of nights
And I felt your glow…it made me feel special

I could flyâ€¦I could sighâ€¦I knew I was safe
I felt like it was the most glorious time I've ever
fell down
Me and youâ€¦the first time I saw you.â€¦ our
vertigo love

                                25. From Me To You

Dear Blair,

            Have you ever looked up at the moon and
            wondered with planets and stars so far
            awayâ€¦she lives in a lonely room? Did
            they tell you not to play with the sun?
            But you had toâ€¦just a human reaction
            to be burnt. Have you sat and tried to
            find sagittarius? Did you shoot the
            arrow into the nothingâ€¦just to watch
            it travel away? I bet there was a day
            you felt a cool breeze off your face and
            you swayed like the trees. I know one
            day you sipped from your cup and felt
            like a growing watered flower. Did you
            stare at the clouds and thinkâ€¦the
            light behind it all was your voice? Have
            you watched the waves crash onto the
            sand and you know like you that beach
            will change a million times? Did you
            look down at the view from the mountains
            and see the cuts in the landscapeâ€¦did
            it remind you of yourself? Do you know
            that all you've seen is inside of you?
            And I must knowâ€¦is there room for me?
            I have seen the same things.

Call me selfishâ€¦but you make me cry every day
Watching you from heavenâ€¦watching you with him
If I recall correctlyâ€¦forever is the word you'd
often say
But you've moved onâ€¦I didn't know forever could
endâ€¦or didn't it begin?

When you look at the skyâ€¦I wish there was a way
for my tears to crash off your beautiful face
But he would surely wipe them away
It's not paradise hereâ€¦it's a lonely place
I am a tortured onlookerâ€¦waiting for the day I see
youâ€¦and scared of what I'll say

Those eyes they told lies
You said I'm all you'll ever want
It felt like honestyâ€¦under those starry skies

Now I am the one dead...and your words and our
memories are what haunts

I didn't ever believe in my heart i was being
deceived
I thought your words to be true…nothing to hide
I didn't think love stops when i cease to breathe
But i guess it's a lesson i learned…from the other
side

Â Â
" The Moon Child And I"

Her welcoming glow poured waterfalls into the
caverns I had inside my heart.
Leaving me floating on her radiance.
Bringing me to new places I had never felt.
Allowing me to see what it was like to be wrapped up
tight inside her illuminating presence.
I had dreamed of this…with eyes wide open…with
her beams of light caressing my troubled shell.
She brought the tide and the waves.
She brought me to my knees…patiently waiting for
her to embrace the passion she had so vividly
brought afloat on this…our sea of love.
She was a child of the moon…and I was a son of the
sun.
With her there…we would blend together…she would
give me her peace…I would share my heated chaos.
And as one…we became the life we had wanted.
We smiled the smiles of those that believe in the
stars and the planets and the paradise within.
We meditated on the magic carpets in the sky.
And soaked in the life given to us by fate.

There had been and always will be a steady beat, a
flashing light, a night aliveâ€¦.as long as she
lives.
For as troubling as reality may seemâ€¦the
fingertips of hers rubbed into my skin the power of
the stars, the serenity of the moonâ€¦.and i....I
just want to love her until I fadeâ€¦into the
sky..into the paradeâ€¦
I will never let her cry without me to burn away the
pain.
And throw it into the sky like confetti.
The ashes of my worst enemyâ€¦her sadness.
Celebrated by the love she gives meâ€¦and the
persistence of a smile on her face.

Â Â
Â Â Â Â "The Light After Us"

Before we metâ€¦I felt as if I had nothing left
With teary eyes I criedâ€¦another stab in the
backâ€¦and it hurt I confess
In my world of darkness and gloomâ€¦I had even
contemplated my own doom
Until you entered the roomâ€¦shining light for me to
bloom

As i felt your presenceâ€¦a small light burned dim
But that light it helped me to lift my head and to
grin
Light and dark togetherâ€¦we are van gogh's starry
night
Alone we are but lonely starsâ€¦together we are the
most beautiful piece of art in sight

As we blended like paint on a canvas new colors came
I felt it in my heartâ€¦I saw a new future in my
brain
I began to shine more and moreâ€¦
each time I saw a message that came from youâ€¦or
when you walked in the door

I hold you highâ€¦so you can shine like you do
The kind of shine that comes only from you
And if there comes a day that you feel you cannot
shineâ€¦
I'll grow dark for the momentâ€¦because you deserve
the lightâ€¦you can have mine

I love you and what you have done for me
You were like the moonâ€¦giving rise to meâ€¦the sea
I want to blend with you foreverâ€¦there could never
be a disaster of us
In my heart I trustâ€¦if we should fadeâ€¦there
would be no light after us

Â Â
Â Â Â Â Â " The Lie Of Gravity"

They said I could never escape this earth less it be
by death or by leaving on a rocketship
But that isn't trueâ€¦I leave this world everytime
my lips touch your lips
I've swayed between the constellationsâ€¦looked down
upon the nationsâ€¦
Because of you with a heart filled with infinite
unsaid words

They claim that there is a great divideâ€¦a heaven
on the other side
But I felt what I know was heaven with youâ€¦a get
away we had hid inside
I felt the pleasure of paradiseâ€¦I had learned a
love blind to those that believed they were too wise
Because of you with a soul whispering sweet
nothing's into the wind

They say to be able to ride the clouds is a story
told in fairy tales
I myself cannot agree as I've sat on them with you
in my armsâ€¦
Feeling the buzz of an awakening loveâ€¦feeling as
if I was lifted above

Because of you an undying hunger for the dish of
happiness you can only serve

They say that I've been crazyâ€¦I guess that in fact
is true
My mind sings songs to the thought of you
A symphony of heartbeats, a hymn to my love
For you have defied the regularâ€¦and you alone
prove the lie of gravity

Â Â
Â Â Â Â Â Â " Petrichor"

Dance with me in the pouring rain
It doesn't matter if we're lost
As long as we're still on our way

Run with me under the tears of the sky
They know the secrets that we've shared
And I think they know the secrets we try to hide

Stand by me in the biggest storm of our lives
It doesn't matter if we drown
As long as it makes us feel alive

Lay with me with our ears to the wet grass
Let's hear our hearts continue to beat
And enjoy the petrichor while we still last

Â Â
"Conversation With The Stars"

You are the satellites to my soulâ€¦why am I about
to give in?
I have not been the kingâ€¦the lion i was meant to
beâ€¦
I look up to youâ€¦.send me a transmission.
Why are all my efforts a tattered messâ€¦disposable
energy.

My salty tears rest on the kneecaps of a wounded
shell.
Oceans behind my nebulized eyes.
Send me a sign that I'll get better…that I'll be
well.
Or will waves pour onto my vessel once more…will I
sink? Will I survive?
The good I've done…not seen. The souls you've sent
have blinded me to purpose.
What is your reason?
Do you send soulmates to hurt us?
Are we the erosion? Are we the avalanche? The
changing of the seasons?
I believe…I feel…I know what you've done…what
you do is real.
So why send a soul to tear down all you helped me
build?
Is their something I don't yet see? Something to be
revealed?
Will a soul come to revive all the confidence the
last one killed?
I hope so…I know so…I just wish I knew the
answer.
I lifted my head to look deep into the night
sky…and saw from afar…
The cure to my emotional cancer…
A falling star.
That's all I needed.

Â Â
Â Â Â Â Â "The Incredible Becoming"

I held the stars in my palms and used their ash to
paint a picture of my future.
No one could understand it but me.
For I was guidedÂ by the lighthouse of the sky
while searching for me in a stormy sea.
And now I found who I was meant to be.
A precise painting.

I stood outside with my hands in the airâ€¦taking
the energy from the moon.
She glowed onto my soul and opened portals into
places only her and I know.
Places only few can go.
The power I now hold has come from ages old.
And now i knowâ€¦what I bringâ€¦cannot be sold.

The sun shined down onto my skin once again.
Petting my very existence.
Reaching into my pores like open holes and feeding
me life and a guarantee.
We cannot look at him or we will not see.
We must feel and witness his actionsâ€¦cherish all
that be.

I reached down and caressed the stream.
watching the movements caused by my touch.
The shape of a moment no one could ever create
again.
The water gracing my fingertipsâ€¦with a puzzle no
one will solve.
The shape of life,the thirst of the heart,all pure
but no one will make the same form twice.

I felt the fire burning inside me.
Like a chaos no one could ever contain.
A dream formed from a spark.
The only light in my dark.
And it will burnâ€¦and I will feelâ€¦it's what makes
us real.

I felt the air blow a breeze into my lungs.
Such a cold airâ€¦but I don't care.
It keeps me alive and brings the scent of a thought
down the road.
Into my faceâ€¦we are oneâ€¦I was never alone.
Into the night we flyâ€¦with blowing leaves at our
back

I reached down and put my hand on the grass.
I felt such a vibrant energy push back.
Life it grabs my handâ€¦it holds it like I'm it's
property.
But we are a teamâ€¦from the dirt until the dirt.

Together we are freeâ€¦.the incredible becoming.

Â Â
Â Â Â Â Â Â Â "The Only Spoon"

I am hungryâ€¦but it's only me and youâ€¦with one
spoon.
You have fed my soulÂ with your smile.
You have fed my heartÂ with your presence.
You have fed my brain with your wisdom.
You have fed my spirit with your strength.
You have fed my muscle with your endurance.
You have fed my happiness with your love.
You have fed my willpower with your guidance.
You have fed my drive with your existence.
You have fed my sight with your visions.
Jordan,aléx,bailee,blayke,â€¦.I'm fullâ€¦you eat
first.

Â Â
Â Â Â Â Â Â "The Blistering Cold"

All the lies you tellâ€¦fall into the well
And destroy all the wishes I had sent
When I look in your eyesâ€¦I despise
And resent the "I love yous" you claimed that you
meant

In the blistering coldâ€¦.I'm growing more bold
I've become numb to the dreams I've been sold

I hope you choke on the words you speak
The ones that make me weak
I hope you know you'll die lonely and alone
Because of all the bad karma your soul holds

In the blistering coldâ€¦I saw with frozen feelings
you break me apart
Just another victim of yoursâ€¦just another heart

You will grow tired and fade… into the bed you
made
Another pathetic liar
And no one will believe a word you say
I will leave your cold heart and enter the fire

In the blistering cold…your hands turned my heart
into ice
I've relocated…here in this warm place…it's nice

Â Â
Â Â Â Â Â Â Â Â Â Â Â Â "My Cloud"

Please walk away from me…don't be so close.
For I am a door closed.
There's no opportunity here…only fear.
A contained room…a lurking gloom…
In my space…a man with no face…no trace…
Closed shades…bloody razorblades...and a packed
suitcase
Just go away.

Don't talk to me…you will not like your response.
For I am a closed book.
There's no knowledge here…only regrets I hold
dear.
Only words never said…only wisdom gone dead.
In my pages…a man ages…a man decays
The breaking apart caused by time…the confusion of
mind…and a chapter unwritten.
Don't try to read me.

Go somewhere else…you won't like the weather by
me.
For this is my cloud.
There's only rain here…and a plane I commandeer.
Only seconds from another storm…only the thunder
to warn.
Under the cloud…the tears of angels and stars…my
death never far.

The saturation of a mental diseaseâ€¦bloody
kneesâ€¦and a weakness in the legs.
You find your ownâ€¦I've made my homeâ€¦I've wrote
my life..I'll die flying through my cloud.

Â Â
Â Â Â Â "Watch Me Bleed"

How could you just sit there and watch me bleed
Can't you say something to heal my wounds
I'm bleeding out all of my own insecurities
And I'm down to my last drop soon

How could you sit there and watch me bleed
With my open heart pouring on the floor
Do you think that makes me weak?
Or is it because you don't love me anymore?

Please don't just watch me bleed
I need your love as a tourniquet
I bleed believing I can't trust anything I see
Because I can't forget

But you just look on and watch me bleed
When you know you're who I need
But you don't need me as you always say
Will you watch me bleed as I walk away?

Â Â
Â Â "A Person You Used To Know"

I've inhaled your words until they created a cancer
on my heart.
Killing the most beautiful part of me.
Until I am but dirt under your shoe.
Buried deep, my seedsâ€¦still blooming flowers of
you.

Dig them up from their roots and take them to your
world to contain them.
Water them with my tears.
Take pictures for show.
A cultivated heartbreakâ€¦yours to bestow.

I was once alive.
Pick the petals of all that's left of me.
Whatever it takes for you to glow.
Until I wiltâ€¦then into the ground I goâ€¦you
refused to help me growâ€¦a person you used to know.

Â Â
Â Â Â Â Â Â " Whispers"

"You deserved better" was but a whisper I heard as I
looked down at the ground.
In a state of confusion.
Could this be? Was this an illusion?
I never looked up at the face that said that to me.

"I'm sure I'll see you again" came another whisper
from out of a fuzzy surrounding.
I was oblivious to the voice. I was in a state of
static mindedness.
Possibly shockâ€¦possibly blindness.

"I'll always love you" whispered a voice almost
right directly beside me.
I didn't lookâ€¦my hands shook. My body felt loose
and light.
What I did seeâ€¦was this right?

A hole was dugâ€¦a casket was being lowered.
People I think I remember embracedâ€¦children cried.
A tombstone with a familiar name in front of
meâ€¦someone has obviously died.

A priest whispered " even though he took his own
lifeâ€¦he will with our prayers for himâ€¦make it to
heaven"
Then all of a sudden it became clearâ€¦

It was meâ€¦I had wanted to be savedâ€¦to be helped
with my fears.

I looked at a woman to my rightâ€¦in tearsâ€¦I try
to calm her and fall through her body as if i am
particles in the air.
"I'm sorry, I'm so sorry" i try to scream but it is
silenced like a brick wall is against my lips.
I can't believe this.

As they all leaveâ€¦I realize that I had made a huge
mistake.
For I am stuck hereâ€¦this my last memoryâ€¦I am not
burningâ€¦I am not a starâ€¦I have not been
delivered.
I will witness my grave with no words ever to be
heardâ€¦with the echo of those people's whispers.

Â Â
Â Â Â Â Â Â Â Â Â Â Â "A Big Black Ribbon"

I no longer know what to believe.
For every second I breathe I want reprieve.
I want retreat from the thoughts still haunting me.
When you look into my eyes what do you see?
All these locked doors inside my mind and I've lost
the keys in a sea of my very own self defeat.
I watched them sink quickly into the deep tied to
the secrets that I keep.
I wonderâ€¦will they ever come back up to breathe?

I sent my message in a bottle onto waters unknown.
I wonder when my words will find a home.
Adrift the waves of change they hope to find their
way but consistently land on hearts of stone.
I hold me high before I let me go.
Not knowing if I'll fall or if I'll float.
The greatest gift I'll never see or know.
Until my death a big black ribbon on my soul.

" The Mark"

I lay here in the indent of a memory
On my left side like you…with my hands holding my
chest like you
The waking and drifting off of all I have left
One last gift
I say goodnight…and I kiss the air
As if it was you…but it never will be
Each and every time I fall asleep I hope you reach
me in my dreams…will this work?
Where have you been?
I miss you
The sun has peaked through the black curtains to
remind me of another day i can't leave what has
kept me close to you.
I have lost weight…i have lost sanity.
The tears so fought against…still they have
poured.
Until behind my eyes a drought has occurred.
In the desert of my soul the only blade of grass has
run out of a chance for fresh morning dew.
And so I am forced to smile…only when I think of
you.
I always think of you.
Our past has echoed in a spot in my brain that
causes euphoria…I sometimes move my hands to reach
for a drink.
But I can't ruin the mark.
The spot on this bed where you died.
So I remain thirsty.
I have to stay here…in case you reach for me…to
let me drink.
To give me my mind back…to let me feel a hunger
other than for your time again.
I today feel as though…hope it is…my last day
laying here waiting for you to come.

No matter the day or night it happens….I'll be here laying in the mark on the bed where you would lay.
Waiting….for the mark to become ours…with hope to see you again.

Â "Dancing In The Flames"

Rosemary she burns and the scent of her flesh speaks to my soul
I am the defected spirit…my body made of stars…my mind a black hole
Yet the calming dies and drum cymbals crash loudly on my peace
The hyenas on my heart…they defeat the lion…they feast

I eat st. John's flower every day
To keep the tears away
Limited in full bloom I assume as I've cried today
The tears…my most faithful companions…yet burdens…they push people away…so we can be alone…but at least they stay

My soul so black…my blood a darker color of red
If only someone would massage away the thoughts in my head
If only I could want to get out of bed
A photographic memory of a future still to come…visions of me dead

Having bipolar disorder is like standing in front of a room on fire…with a twisted version of gravity pulling you close enough to feel the pain
Your tears not enough to put the fire out…but you cry…and you try and try and try…you're insane
You have no choice…you can't escape…it will never change.

Your only choiceâ€¦to cry until you are nothing but ashâ€¦or to laugh as you lose yourself while dancing in the flames.

Â "Lightning Kite"

One day, someone will look for me.
But I will be long gone.
Drifting upon the winds of change with the wings of age on my shoulders.
I will cast a light upon the shadow of grieving.
All that will remain will be a reflection of my storms.
The tears will break the smiles down.
And the rain will fall upon the saddened onlookers.
Why? How? When?
No one really knows.
But I am a temporary gift to humanity.
A blink upon the eye of existence.
A shattered bone upon the mass of life's body.
A memory of a soul and a thought held tight to be let go.
I am the sand castle and the high tide.
I will fade like a ghost into the walls of invisibility.
To become fluorescent in the sunshine.
To become a strand among the thread.
Digested by the greatest fear and swallowed by those with my name in their timelines.
To floatâ€¦to let go by force.
To run out of options.
I am death and when I come to myself for takingâ€¦
I'll be another story forgotten.
A kite in the lightning.

Â "The Sagittarius And The Suffocation"

I looked into her eyes and saw a heart so big, even though, she had been lied to and used.
And I looked even deeper into her soul and saw the bad choices she chose.
Such a beautiful creature that wants to be free in a world contained in a sphere.
So I cried tears for her in private so my sadness for her wouldn't show…I wonder if she looks in my eyes she would know.

She told me she didn't need me. It made her feel more comfortable to not need anyone.
It must be hard to hold a wall up so high without it attached to anything.
I held her as she cried on a few occasions…at other times she shoots her arrows aimlessly into her sky and sea.
I fear,as a lion, one day she will turn her arrow to me.

She says I suffocate her…but i don't try to
I try to keep my distance when she needs me to
But I'm drawn to her like an insect to the light
I want to be her everything and i know i never will be

So now…as we have to part ways…I wonder if she realizes that to make her happy I'll go away.
With a saddened heart and broken soul.
And each step I take away from her breathes more life into her…
And each step I take away from her…I die a little more of suffocation.

Â "See You In Heaven"

Hey, how are you up there?
I'm not so good down here.
When it rains it pours and when it floods I'll
drown.
I was thinking of you alot lately.
If you were here I'd have your friendship as a
lifejacket.
But you're gone and I miss youâ€¦and I miss me.
The stones have been thrown.
And I gathered them into a huge collection.
I don't know what to do with them now.
If you were here you'd pick them up and throw them
back for me.
I wouldâ€¦but I don't have the energy.
It seems I don't have anyone to stand against my
enemies.
I'm going through changes and I've burnt bridges
without crossing them first.
So I'm stuck on the side that they live onâ€¦and I
can't swim.
You'd love me anyway.
You'd make me smile.
But you're gone for good and I now laugh with my
shadow.
After awhile it grows old and tiresome.
I don't feel alive.
Not like I did when you were here.
I'm not sure how much longer i could survive.
But I do hope that paradise is all it was told to us
it was.
I'll fight because you told me to.
I'll try to rise once again and wait on fate.
And try to believe that I'll see you again.
I miss you.
I hope you're happy where you are.
And if it exists I'll see you in heaven.

Â "League
Of The Beautifully Broken"

The heartbreak had me at a sad silence.
I cried into the emptiness.

A million visions floated from my dark aura into the universe contained in the small room.
My breath was rare and limited.
Each exhale leaving out the hope I was told I should have.
My soul dug deep the shovel into the bones of happiness.
Every light destroyedâ€¦a group of memories to watch the burial.
Songs played in my ears I've never heard before.
Their source I'll never know.
The cheap rope is not worth the tie.
The descent is the highlight.
A passionate action left in a heartless world.
The trees,the moon, the dirt all holding more smiles than the souls I've witnessed.
My words a testament to a crack in the process of life.
Leaking a wounded little boy,a hurting young man, an ancient soul.
The white roses will bloom where I rot.
And should I be ashamed?
For creating something beautiful from my demise.
I fall and will it cause a rise?
Sometimes the disappearance of a presence or a foreverâ€¦
Lifts up the rest.
And so an invisible memorial will be built in their minds.
My name to join the league of the beautifully broken.

Â Â
Â Â Â Â "Sincerely, The Lion"

I have hidden in the shadows quietly for too long. I have to attack now. Forgive my unpleasant demeanor and rageful approach. But there's too much left unsaid and not enough acted upon. First, to the Christians of modern dayâ€¦be what you say you are. It is already apparent to me that your "god" is heavily fabled more than factual. But if you are to preach to the weak to give strength,then be what your book asks you to be. It says a man is not to lie with another man. So you cannot be Christian and support homosexuality. Or hence you support homosexuality and not your jesus. Also, stop the judging of those with dissimilar beliefs. They do not walk your path. But they too have a path. Being humble and informative would shine brighter than a cold shoulder that reminds me of a stone unturned with nothing but poisonous serpents beneath.

To those deceitful and full of lies. I have a lesson for you. Each lie you tell is a house with a Hornets nest on the porch. If the wind should shake it loose you best not be present and unsheltered. Honesty hurts much less than a pretend friendly action. You are weak in the heart. You are cold in your bones. You are an easy target for me. I have a handful of tricks to your aired out assault. You will lay in a bed of loneliness among the rest of your equals. And I the honest will smile and feast upon your corpse.

Last but not least…to those in need…if you need a home…a friendly face…my pride is here. I will bend nature to my will. I will feed the famine and give water to the thirsty. I will,if need be, violently dominate the ones who confront your needs. I will conquer with the moon at my back and the sun on my skin. I will reign in such a way that the dead trees smile and the fresh grapes gather at my feet. I wish you all the best…blessed be.

                                        "The Tree
                                        Swing"

"You look so beautiful today. Just like you did in those golden days. We would sit under this tree and swing seasons away. Do you remember that? I'm sure you do" I say as I look over at your smiling face.

I was so proud to have you. To know you loved me and
that I was the one you chose. And here we are. I'm
so old now. All these years and you still live
inside my heart. And at certain times of the day you
reside in my arms.

They never thought we'd make it. That the obstacles
of life would conquer our love. That anything could.
But I know more than anyone that we are inseparable
and unbreakable.
Look at us. Look at you. Still so gorgeous and so
funny. Still taking my breath away more than any
woman ever could.

I push my old legs out to send the swing in motion.
Holding your hand I look over at you with a look of
love and passion.
I can still see. At 90 years of age. I can still see
you. I can still feel you. Nothing has faded. The
paradox of life was just that. I told you I'd love
you forever. And we are still in our favorite spot.
Swinging. Among the field of sunflowers. Swinging
more. Among the doubts. Swinging so high. In the
place we belong. Together.

"Jimmy…James…time to get off the swing."says a
man with a smile on his face.
"But I was just talking to Blair. She still loves
me. We're having the time of our lives." I reply.
"Well you know Blair will still be there tomorrow
during recreation time" he replies.
"Yes she will never leave. We said forever." I say
as I smile.
I turn and I wave at the tree swing.
"I love you baby" I say.

 I say it to the memory of a love. Of the person
 that passed away years ago. And then I go into the
 nursing home. Still in love. Still believing. And
 until the day I die. Every day. I spend my free
 time on the tree swing.

                                        "I Was Here"

I waited until one of his favorite kinds of nights.
When the stars were shining bright outside the
window I filled the tub.
I've been by his side.
 So much that i was the best part of him.
But he will never see it.
He barely acknowledges me.
I watched him struggle and when he did he asked me
to be better.
To step up to help him feel good.
Sometimes I fail.
I can't be perfect.
He cursed me.
He said he lost me.
But I was there.
He just didn't recognize it.
I watched him drink his wine and watch his stars.
His anger and sadness created so much torment.
I saw within him his potential.
But,his one sided mind,it blocked me from giving him
all I could.
And now I'll lay in this tub.
I'll show him for never treating me like he should
have.
With razorblades just like he did when he was
younger.
I was there to see it all.
But never was I good enough to help him stop.
I had to make this decision.
And so I dig the razorblades into my veins.
And I bleed.
He will be nothing without me.
And before I pass out I draw on the wall words with
my blood.
I am Jimmy's talent.
'I was here'

                                        "Love My
                                        Scars"

You see these scars on my arm?

They're proof that there's more to a face than a name and a smile.
Each scar tells a story that never leaves my lips.
They signify the days I had to let the pain leak out because I couldn't keep it in.
There's been days I had been at the bottom so long I made it my home.
I built my own castle of sadness on the floors of a troubled youth.
I was confused.
I still am.
But I learned to let it all leak out through the ink in my pen.
I wonder if people think my sickness makes me lesser than them.
On certain days it's a gem.
I'm manic and nothing in the world could stop me.
I stand on top of the universe and love harder than anyone possibly can.
Then with no known sign I fall.
Hitting every insecurity or worthless thought I feel on the way down.
And I cry.
Unstable but still loving,still caring,just feeling every feeling there is to feel.
It's unreal.
How it grips my mind and forces me.
Mentally raped by a disease every day of my life and I feel like I'm still and yet jogging in place.
I know they see the expression.
I can't hide my face I have a woman to love and children to raise.
So I pace.
Trying to fight this son of a gun with a knife.
The sharpness of my wits will never beat it.
It's too conceited to let me win and even if I defeat it it still will squeeze my heart from within.
Me and this virus this parasite we are enemies.
So no wonder I've harmed myself.
The days I have the will to let me be happy the chemicals won't let me.
They have overrun this establishment and now I serve them bad days on a platter.

So I just wait on my next moment of temporary
happiness.
I will love it when it comes.
And I appreciate the seratonin and dopamine that
some create chemistry with in my brain.
To,even for moments, take away my pain.
I will always be this lesser than best version of
me.
So I askâ€¦just love my scars anyway.

                              "I Saw Your
                              Reflection"

I see you being too concerned with what you're not.
How will you ever know what you are?
With your head down and a mind in the stars.
I hope you know one day.
I hope you get that far.

I see you thinking that everyone is against you.
How will you ever see who's by your side?
With your fists clenched and nowhere to hide.
They're not invisible and you're not blind.
I suggest you open your eyes up wide.

I see you trembling in a cold cruel world.
Have you forgotten the warmth your soul holds?
Filled with bitterness and having nowhere to go.
I hope your light shines from within.
I hope you let it show.

I see you struggling and wanting to end it all.
But how will you know what might have been?
With a dying spirit and a long lost grin.
I hope you stick around to see.
I hope you win.

I found myself in the hot shower thinking of the
observations of you in my head.

I stepped out and wiped the steam off the glass to
make it more clear.
I saw your reflection in the mirror.

                              "Have A Heart"

I sit here next to your unconscious body as you're
filled with tubes.
There's a doctor in my ear telling me that without a
new heart you'll never make it.

I think if all the times I did nothing but love you.
And you never did love me the same.
There were so many times I looked to you for
reassurance and you told me I was weak.
Or the moments I looked to you for comfort and you
gave me even more discomfort.
But I still and always did hold you up so high.
On your bad days i felt the raindrops from all your
dark clouds.

Sometimes I've wondered if you even love me at all.
If I'm in your life for some sort of selfish reason.
But there were days you shined towards me.
Those were my favorite daysâ€¦maybe of my whole
life.

So I went home to our lonely house.
Scared.
Scared for you and for what I will do if you can't
be saved.
But this house is as empty as my soul would be
without you.

So I did what any person would do for the person he
loves.
I put the gun in my mouth.
I pulled the trigger.
Leaving a Butterfly of brains on the wall.

I had placed the 911 call right before I did it
though.

And I left a note.

"Hey baby,

> I'm not sure if you loved me.
> But just in case you did and
> because it doesn't change how
> much I love you…I left you
> what I always told you was yours
> anyway…here…have my heart.
> Goodbye.

"Our
Escape"

I think we should stand one-legged on top of the
telephone poles with our arms spread out to our
sides.
We should imagine that the wind strikes fire to our
invisible feathers.
That it drifts us to a world with no war,no hate, no
negative status.
Where we could believe we've gotten away from the
madness.

We could pretend we made a universe with our
marbles.
And we live there.
We elevated into the colors like a hot air balloon.
Above all the jet streams…away from the poverty
and sadness.

We have woke in fields of dandelions and daisies
with the sun on our face.
We picked off the petals and found we love each
other and we blew the whiskers into the summer sky.
They gave us the power to heal.
We are the heroes and have avoided the mind
controlling media.

We have hand crafted a world free of storms and
disease.
We swing from our moons on giant swings.
Placing our stars where we wish like young,free
picassos.
We have departed from what holds us to our ways.

And then we turn on the news.
We look out our windows.
We stare at our phones.
Only in our minds have I found our escape.

"My Aura's Aura"

I wonder if the ashes of the stars cover the inside
of each drop of blood inside of me.
Do they help me to shine on days when the night and
I are the same?
I think they help me be vibrant in times I need
guidance.
If they fallâ€¦I fall.
Kismet waiting.

There's a planet circulating around my heart.
Watching it thrive like the sun.
Giving life to it.
Many flowers have bloomed and wilted there.
Still it beats heat throughout.

My soul is like the ocean.
Waves upon waves of past lives.
Rising with the moon.
Sailed upon by adventurers.
Many secrets buried in the deepest of it's depths.

When people say we are all alikeâ€¦I don't agree.
Not many think like me.
And all they see is my shell's aura.
But I know my Aura's aura is the universe.
We are not the same.

"The Glow"

I've crawled so far to reach you.
Breathing in this pain and exhaling my terror.
Stuck behind these walls.
Fixed inside these bones.
A lonely light dimmed by a darker shadow.
I open up my mouth and scream.
It is muffled by traffic.
I am choked by my lack of being myself.
Or loving who I am now.
Or liking what today has given me.
A cactus on my tonsils.
Dreading what tomorrow brings.
I've got kneecaps exposed from the rough travelling.
Making my way to you.
My memories are blurry.
Some smiling faces clenching freshly sharpened
knives.
Their heart rupturing eyes concentrating on my back.
While others had watched.
They laughed.
They belittled me.
They put me down for wearing my heart on my sleeve.
And so I burned my sleeves away.
Until I was a naked mess.
My fingernails broken and hurting.
And so I've made my way to you.
Do you see this darkness that covers me?
Love me.
Dig your hands in deep and tear me open.
Violently if you must.
Until you once again see the glow.
Can you see me shine?
Am I good enough now?
Then save me.

Come lie with me in this field of high grass.
Us 5 can talk about life,smileâ€¦.laugh.
Do you see the birds up in the trees?
More determined,more happy,singing and being more
free than you or me.

Youâ€¦.you made me keep writing. You encouraged me
when I was going to put the pen down. I took your
advice and no one knows how you woke me up. I
wantedâ€¦so badlyâ€¦to see you with a love that
looked at you with the beauty your soul was. The big
baby,the big teddy bearâ€¦.my friend. You motivated
me one time when no one could. I had fresh blood on
a page one time while you messaged me. You told me
that I was a person that inspired you and that I
should keep going on. You made my dreams come alive.
Thank you nick Dolci for being a person on days that
no one else was.

Youâ€¦.your father died and we drank jack daniels
behind the library. You cried. You told me your
insecurities and your pains. I spoke with a
knowledge of youth. You almost shot me in the head
accidentally with your fathers gun. And we listened
to incubus and spoke of what our dreams were. You
told me not to speak of it all. I never did. Larry
wagner... thank you for being a stranger that became
a friend in such few moments.

Youâ€¦ you and I were a special request from earth.
A connection of the stars. We were not attracted to
each other. Not by a physical form. But a chemistry
that people deny. You were so young. It hurts me so
badly that you asked for me to help you and I gave
you my number. With no call. Only a message that
said you're gone. When i know you saved my life when
my mother died. You were the first and only one who
made me who i am now. Thank you so much for
existing. I'll never let them forget it carissa
sandefer.

Youâ€¦thank you for making me a hero. You told me I
could. You raised me to be a man better than I was
while you were still on this earth. I hate myself
every day for being how I was. Your death was my
birth. No one knows like I do. No one will ever
experience what I did. Natureâ€¦it touched meâ€¦the
stars embraced meâ€¦the sun spoke and the moon
sobbed with me. Your beliefs were correct. It saved
me. Though I wish I could have been by your side.
Taking your last breath. Everything I know is
because of you. I remember your face more often than
I want to. It brings tears. But I'll be specialâ€¦I
was to youâ€¦thank you mom.

I look up and we could smile.
With no one near us for miles.
We are the birds now.
We are whatever we want to be somehow.
You could leave this earth but know you'll always
beâ€¦.
In the hiding place in my mindâ€¦where you'll never
be gone to me.

                                   "The Best One Of Our
                                   Lives"

We often ponder why do people stay together?
They say "if you're unhappy then leave".
I've been unhappy with my children,my girlfriend,and
my parents.
I didn't leave them. Why?
Because I'll have bad days of my own.
Should they walk away from my sad or miserable
state?
Should we abandon all bad times?
Would we ever learn about ourselves or from each
other if we did?
I keep my mind from being caged by running free with
the animals I associate with.

To disown a partnership over temporary discomfort is
a weakness and a seeking of the easy way.
Which makes sense to do if you never think you'll
fall on your own.
If you've walked away from everyone who will be
there for you?

When a couple does bad everyone thinks that
happiness only exists in their earlier days.
Butâ€¦noâ€¦you just know what your partner is
capable of.
Who cares who caused the coming down from that high?
Time, understanding,integrity,faithfulness,and
communication breathe life into anyone.
It's about being strong.
But not just for yourself.
For the bondâ€¦the United actions of soulsâ€¦the
connection of hearts.
You just have to know there will be alot of good and
bad days and nights.
But that one day,under a moon or sun, we'll have
the best one of our lives.
It will be worth it.

                              "My Art"

I was the conductor.
I'd wave my baton at this wonderful orchestra I had
assembled.
Each of them playing an instrument.
Each of them with their very own fire.
Every seat was filled with a person so eager to
see,to hear,and to feel the presence of them.
My very own orchestra.

My very own special violinist.
He was so sorrowful and people had weeped at the way
he spoke with the echoes of his pain bouncing off
the walls.
But all of them unique and special to me.

I lifted the baton up high and low to guide them.
To let them know I was always watching and
listening.
And judging.

They worked so hard.
It tugged at my heart.
It consumed my soul.
But at some point I lost control of them.
They didn't watch me.
They didn't let me lead them.
They just closed their eyes and did what they do.

And on this very night, with an arena full of eager
listeners, they played a song I never instructed
them to play.
I was confused.
Angry.
Disappointed.
Am i no longer the one in control?

And so i opened up my eyes.
On an empty stage I stood.
The arena also empty.
The only echo a drip of rain coming from a hole in
the roof.
The orchestra had been my moods.
But just to be professional.
I took a bowâ€¦"thank you.have a good night" I said
to a lonely building.
And as i walked off stage a single tear fell from my
eye.

"Heart Shaped World"

With so many people striving to be the chiefâ€¦the
onlookers with termite infested wooden hearts are
avoided.
A cotton paper running our mindsâ€¦ robots with
poison in our blood to deal with our day.

A like icon gives people another idea of who they
really are.
I wonder will there be a day that comes before I die
that the world is silent while typing their
forgotten voice.
Will all human feelings disappear into a wire?
Will affection be virtually duplicated?

Those that breathe in the fresh air no longer value
it.
But some people don't have that air.
They breathe in sand storms filled with molecular
death.
I almost forgot, while drinking some cool spring
water,that there are people on earth hoping for a
chance to drink acid rain from small mud puddles.

Addiction is everywhere.
It's like they play pool with the stars.
Hittingâ€¦.reguiding their future into a black hole.
by using the eight ball.
Butterflies fly from that very hole and into the
sun.
To burn for the sister that never will be the same
after playing that very game.

We have binoculars to our eyes as our children play
in the street.
A stranger with murderous or sexual needs may tear
our blooming flowers from their roots.
Peaceful souls are clutching guns.
Imprisoned on our own planet.
By the evil world we have allowed.

I sit in the darkest of rooms with my energy
sobbing.
For I cannot change our course on my own.
And I sympathize with all of you for what I know is
to come.
May the stars be merciful on the rest of your
existence in this life.

I am going to encourage that you use your brain and
heart as often as possible.

Although we are all outnumbered by the snakes and
vultures.
We can hug who we love,be grateful for what we have,
keep a clear mind,our heads high,and hope our
children watch.
That they change this place into a heart shaped
world.

"Am I A Monster?"

Do one last thing for me before you go away forever
Pry your heart from my closed hand
For I have hurt it againâ€¦by being myself
For being what I've been made to be by my past

My bloodshot eyes are tired from having to observe
all around me
Because of fearâ€¦I have to watch
Because I will not let someone hurt me
I believeâ€¦I will be prepared I will know

Hold your hands over your ears for the many
questions I ask
I ask to ease my heart
But in my mind I already have the answer
You too do not love meâ€¦not enoughâ€¦just like
everyone.

And so you hurt
And I do not notice
I have to prevent myself from pain
I have to live with fists clenched breaking my own
heart with thoughts

And every time I am this way you die inside
I wonder when I became this
And how many hearts have I destroyed because I
cannot trust
Am I a monster?

"What A Sky"

On a summer day I sat alone.
Feeling the rays of the sun touching my skin.
A green and black butterfly hovering above my
head...eventually landing on my shoulder.
I gently put the butterfly in my hand.
And I held it up high.
Staring at the sun through a butterfly's wing.
I saw the truth.
I saw the beauty.
The green turning to pink.
The black turning to white.
The hairs silver.
Then the butterfly flew away into it's own world.
I wonder if it remembered me for even a second.
If it could recall the moment we spent.

To my right three birds graced the sky.
Soaring in the air so free.
Feeling the wind cool their feathers.
The sun creating silhouettes.
They were angels to me.
And one flew down and landed on a nearby tree.
Maybe too tired from it's flight.
Maybe enjoying the day like me.

Straight forward I saw a plane.
Filled with people going somewhere.
Maybe looking out their windows at the sun as well.
Admiring the life below.
The man on his porch staring back at them.
A silent wave.
A connecting gaze.
All in the warmth.

It occurred to me,
That I am them all.
The butterfly,the birds, the people in the plane,
All of us living this day in the same snapshot.
The sun our photographer.
And I believe we all posed well.
What a sky.

"Last One Left"

When you cry they all come running to wipe your
tears away.
They hold protests with picket signs rallying
against your abuser.
They care so much about your feelings.
They bring you gifts so they might have the chance
to see your smile.
All they want is for you to be happy.
For you to stop doubting yourself.
They walk beside you just to lift your head when it
falls.
They tell you how much you matter to them.
They say that this world would not be the same
without you.
That you are an inspiration.
The fire you desire has a group standing around it
fanning the flames.
So many friends exist in your life.
There is no hostile ignorance.
There is no deceitful silence.
This is trueâ€¦when you are the last one left on
earth.

"Worth"

There I was face down in the gutter.
With no one paying attention to me.
No one would pick me up.
No one cared that I lie there at all.
They stepped over me and on me.
Maybe if I was biggerâ€¦.if I could help them get
the things they want.
But they only seem to care when my head's up.

Or when I'm shining bright.
I feel very hard on myself.
As time goes by I become more and more obsolete.
I've heard them talk as they walk byâ€¦.I have no value.
Then one day i heard a voice "Hey mom, it's a penny"
A little boy picked me up and tossed me into his pocket.
I'm glad he saw my worth.

                    "When The Night Comes(A Letter
                    To Blair)"

In starting this I have to clarify and admit that
you scare me to death. In fact I don't think I fear
anything reallyâ€¦ except being hurt by you. You
came during a change in my course and you have been
the light beside me and inside of me ever since. I
have fallen in love with all of you. Your outer
beauty and your heart and soul. I still have the
same goal in life. To make you smile. Until I die
that's what I want. To me it would be the greatest
gift I've ever received from our universe. Just
simply, the privilege of being the one that makes
you smile. I know life will throw us punches. I know
there will be plenty of days that we run out of
things to say and sit in a silence some would find
discomforting. I know days will go by
unbalanced,stressful,painful,as well as
joyous,thrilling,exciting, wonderful days also.
There will be days that we will have to pick each
other up. There will be days that we are unable to.
But what I know in my soul is that we won't let each
other down. My love for you is real. I know this
when I think of you. There's days that I drive
myself crazy feeling like I'm going to lose you. I
worry that I make you unhappy. It tears a hole into
my future. And my dreams disappear. Then you hug me
and you tell me I make you happy. And it makes me
feel like my purpose is still intact. My love for
you is different. It's not just another I love you

when i say it. Because every day I am dedicated to you. To your happiness,to your smile, to standing next to you whenever you feel lonely. I want that for the rest of my breaths. Every day. And I just want you to promise that you feel the same. So I can rest my headâ€¦.when the night comes.

"Taking Your Breath Away"

Let the dirt under my nails remind youâ€¦
Of the sand my hands held you let slip through the creases of my fingers.
Our time is up.

Let the earth still stuck to this shovel help you recallâ€¦
That I once believed you and I were magic.
It had nothing to do with you.

As I inhale a tear from the top of my lip i think of the memoriesâ€¦.
The times i felt without you i was not whole and that you were the reason i was special.
I no longer believe that though.

The bitter words I mutter as I put you in the ground still alive should be a displayâ€¦.
Of the frustrations I have,of the disappointment you caused, of my realization that you waited for me to be sad so you could shine.
I've made the decisionâ€¦my mind will no longer lead me.

As you metaphorically gasp for air let it be knownâ€¦
I know you,my pen, and our 8 collections ends here.
I laugh as I cry.

I fix my collar…you can't see it though can you…can you somehow feel my smirk.
I look up at the sky and drink the salty tear filled rain.
This is a new beginning.

I take off my shoes and sit on the couch and I know.…
Ink will flow from the next two seasons.
And I will not be responsible for any of it.

I open the window….the petrichor fills my nostrils.
A small wind blows through the screen.
I smell the zephyr…straight from the clouds…filled with the scent of stars and sun rays.

Be ready.